COSORI AIR FRYER COOKBOOK UK

1200 days of Crispy, Delicious and Easy to Fry, Bake, Grill Recipes for

Your Cosori Air Fryer

DIANE J. BRANCH

Table of Contents

Introduction

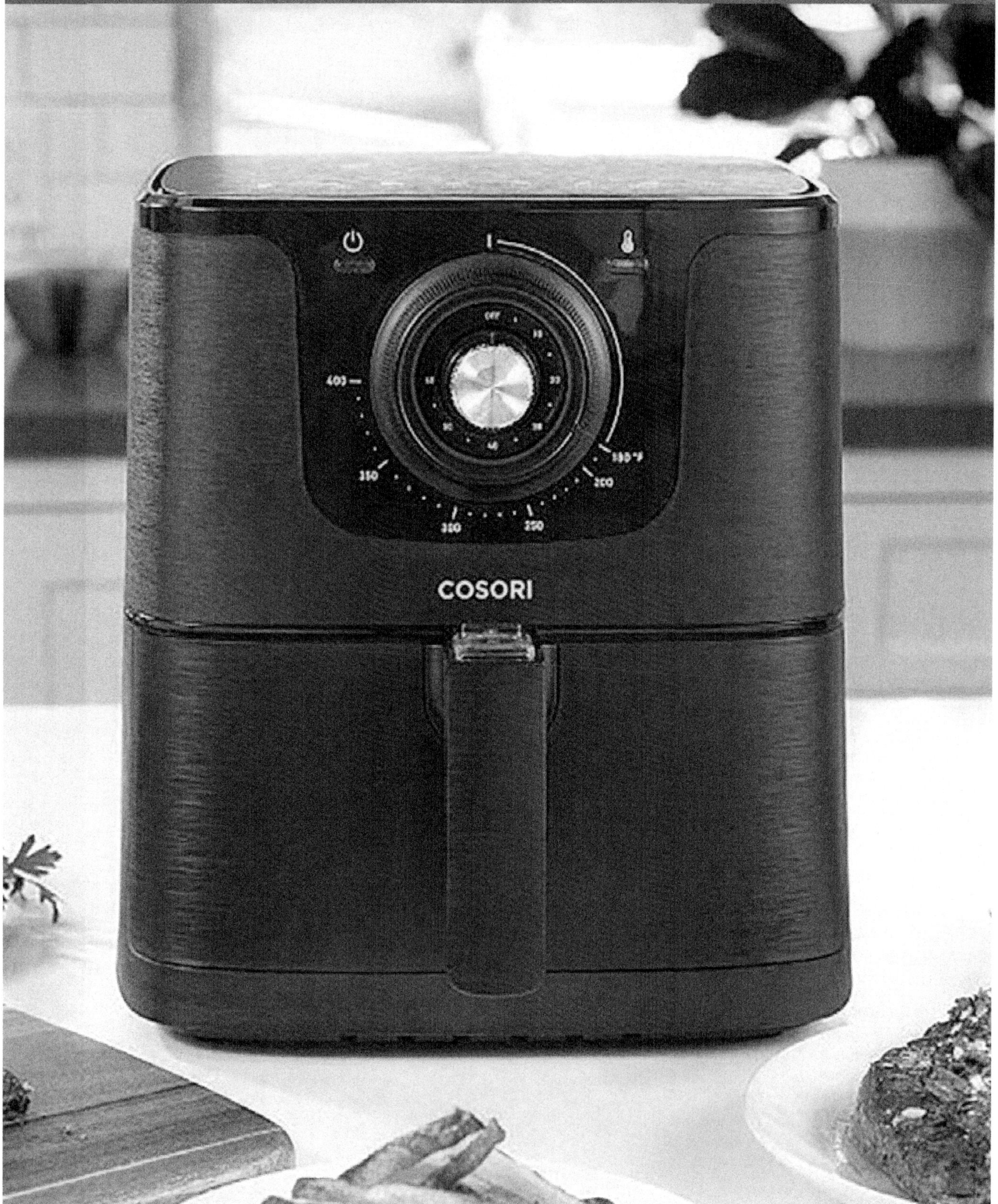

Does a picture-perfect kitchen catch your fancy? Do you also love cooking and experimenting with new recipes? Then, really, you need an air fryer!

My opinion about air fryers was that "they were conventional ovens and nothing more," and since I had an oven, I didn't bother about having another countertop that would occupy extra space. But was I wrong? Well, you guessed right!

Aside from the fact that air fryers are time efficient since they take less time to cook, they also help reduce calorie intake because they need only little oil to deliver efficiently. Before deep-diving into the details of this cookbook, what about familiarizing ourselves with what exactly air fryers are, why you need one, the various types available, and every other detail you need to know?

An air fryer is a cooking appliance placed on the counter that uses a heating function and a strong fan to circulate hot air. Air fryers make food crispy outside and moist and soft inside without frying.

Chapter 1
Basics of COSORI Air Fryer

An air fryer bakes and roasts with lesser oil than a deep fryer uses. As opposed to its name, an air fryer doesn't fry foods; instead, its powerful fan blows hot air around the food in the basket.

Types of Air Fryers

Air fryers have different shapes, materials, noise production, temperature, thickness, and wash tolerance. They vary in functionality; for instance, you can bake, grill, broil and toast foods with some, while some only have single functions. The different types of air fryers include:

CYLINDRICAL BASKET AIR FRYER

The heat of this kind of air fryer is from the top, with its heat blowing down the heat to ensure thorough cooking and crispy result. The cylindrical air fryers are portable and heat up faster than other air fryers. The shortcoming of this kind of air fryer is that it has a single function as opposed to an oven air fryer that can grill, roast, fry, and broil.

It is best for a single user because it can take a maximum of 3 quarts of food and would necessitate cooking in batches during extensive cooking.

BASKET AIR FRYER

As its name suggests, the basket air fryer cooks food in a basket. The basket has a handle that makes carrying and flipping at intervals during cooking possible. Unlike other air fryers, you must constantly pay attention to what you are cooking to toss or flip the fries. The basket air fryer has a considerably long-life span because the fewer parts reduce the risk of losing some parts.

OVEN AIR FRYER

The oven air fryer is similar to the cylindrical basket air fryer. However, as opposed to it, the oven air fryer has racks that hold a crisper and a baking tray. In addition, unlike the cylindrical basket air fryer, the oven air fryer cooks in silence and has the feature of cooking, broiling, baking, grilling, frying, toasting, etc.

Although the oven air fryer occupies a larger countertop space in the kitchen and takes more time to preheat, it has a higher cooking capacity as an average oven air fryer can cook 25 food quarts.

PADDLE AIR FRYER

The paddle air fryer is very convenient since you don't have to turn it at intervals to ensure even cooking.
The paddle air fryer turns food automatically without human intervention. The paddle of the air fryer is detachable to create more room for more extensive cooking. The paddle air fryer can cook various kinds of food, such as fries, curries, frozen foods, mixed vegetables, risotto, etc.

Choosing the kind of air fryer you want depends on your preference, what you need in your kitchen, and your budget.

Why Should You Have an Air Fryer.

- It Promotes Healthy Cooking: The significant advantage of an air fryer is the use of minimal oil which promotes healthy cooking and eating because of the calorie reduction in food. Therefore, it is a suitable replacement for deep-fried food, which are only sometimes healthy.
- It Is Fast, Safe, and Easy to Handle: Many people opt to eat out because of the stress and the time that home cooking requires. Although air fryers don't cook all kinds of food, they cook enough variety of foods within a short time to avoid monotonic eating and wasting time. It means you eat varieties and spend little time while home cooking, saving you the extra cost of eating out.
- It Makes Food Crispier and Crunchier: Foods made with air fryers are crunchier and crispier outside and tender inside, which makes it enjoyable rather than oil-soaked fries. Your food only requires a sprinkle of little oil, and you will get a fantastic result.

Trust me, this is not an exhaustive list of advantages. But hopefully, they help you see even more reasons getting your air fryer wasn't a bad idea!

Tips for Using an Air Fryer

1. Preheat your air fryer before placing your food.
2. Use a kitchen oil sprayer to spray oil on your food rather than pouring.
3. An aluminum foil sling makes placing and lifting the baking pan in the air fryer easier.
4. while cooking fatty foods, Add water to the air fryer drawer
5. Don't overcrowd the basket to avoid uneven crisping and browning
6. If you are not using the paddle air fryer, flip the food when the cooking is half done.
7. Use toothpicks to pin light foods to prevent being blown around.
8. To get more browning results, spray the food with oil halfway into the cooking.
9. Remove the air fryer basket from the drawer before taking your food out.
10. Don't put the hot drawer on your countertop.
11. Clean the basket and the drawer thoroughly after every use.
12. You can use the air fryer to dry itself by putting it on for 2 to 3 minutes.

One of the loveliest decisions I made for my kitchen and cooking inquisitiveness is to include an air fryer. It made cooking easier and more convenient.
Enough of the prepping; let's get into the real deal – the best recipes you can prepare using your Cosori Air Fryer!

Chapter 2
Staples

Buttery Mushrooms

Prep time: 8 minutes | Cook time: 30 minutes | Makes about 1½ cups

- 1 pound (454 g) button or cremini mushrooms, washed, stems trimmed, and cut into quarters or thick slices
- ¼ cup water
- 1 teaspoon flake salt or ½ teaspoon fine salt
- 3 tablespoons unsalted butter, cut into pieces, or extra-virgin olive oil

1. Place a large piece of tin foil on the sheet pan. Place the mushroom pieces in the middle of the foil. Spread them out into an even layer. Pour the water over them, season with the salt, and add the butter. Wrap the mushrooms in the foil.
2. Select Roast. Set temperature to 160°C and set time to 15 minutes. Press Start to begin preheating.
3. Once the unit has preheated, place the pan into the Air Fryer.
4. After 15 minutes, remove the pan from the Air Fryer. Transfer the foil packet to a cutting board and carefully unwrap it. Pour the mushrooms and cooking liquid from the foil onto the sheet pan.
5. Select Roast. Set temperature to 180°C and set time to 15 minutes. place the pan into the Air Fryer. Press Start to begin preheating.
6. After about 10 minutes, remove the pan from the Air Fryer and stir the mushrooms. Return the pan to the Air Fryer and continue cooking for 5 to 15 more minutes, or until the liquid is mostly gone and the mushrooms start to brown.
7. Serve immediately.

Shawarma Seasoning

Prep time: 5 minutes | Cook time: 0 minutes | Makes about 1 tablespoon

- 1 teaspoon smoked paprika
- 1 teaspoon cumin
- ¼ teaspoon turmeric
- ¼ teaspoon flake salt or ⅛ teaspoon fine salt
- ¼ teaspoon cinnamon
- ¼ teaspoon allspice
- ¼ teaspoon red pepper flakes
- ¼ teaspoon freshly ground black pepper

1. Stir together all the ingredients in a small bowl.
2. Use immediately or place in an airtight container in the pantry.

Garlic Tomato Sauce

Prep time: 15 minutes | Cook time: 30 minutes | Makes about 3 cups

- ¼ cup extra-virgin olive oil
- 3 garlic cloves, minced
- 1 small onion, chopped (about ½ cup)
- 2 tablespoons minced or puréed sun-dried tomatoes (optional)
- 1 (28-ounce / 794-g) can crushed tomatoes
- ½ teaspoon dried basil
- ½ teaspoon dried oregano
- ¼ teaspoon red pepper flakes
- 1 teaspoon flake salt or ½ teaspoon fine salt, plus more as needed

1. Heat the oil in a medium saucepan over medium heat.
2. Add the garlic and onion and sauté for 2 to 3 minutes, or until the onion is softened. Add the sun-dried tomatoes (if desired) and cook for 1 minute until fragrant. Stir in the crushed tomatoes, scraping any brown bits from the bottom of the pot. Fold in the basil, oregano, red pepper flakes, and salt. Stir well.
3. Bring to a simmer. Cook covered for about 30 minutes, stirring occasionally.
4. Turn off the heat and allow the sauce to cool for about 10 minutes.
5. Taste and adjust the seasoning, adding more salt if needed.
6. Use immediately.

Lemon Anchovy Dressing

Prep time: 5 minutes | Cook time: 0 minutes | Makes about ⅔ cup

- ½ cup extra-virgin olive oil
- 2 tablespoons freshly squeezed lemon juice
- 1 teaspoon anchovy paste
- ¼ teaspoon flake salt or ⅛ teaspoon fine salt
- ¼ teaspoon minced or pressed garlic
- 1 egg, beaten

1. Add all the ingredients to a tall, narrow container.
2. Purée the mixture with an immersion blender until smooth.
3. Use immediately.

Teriyaki Sauce

Prep time: 5 minutes | Cook time: 0 minutes | Makes ¾ cup

- ½ cup soy sauce
- 3 tablespoons honey
- 1 tablespoon rice wine or dry sherry
- 1 tablespoon rice vinegar
- 2 teaspoons minced fresh ginger
- 2 garlic cloves, smashed

1. Beat together all the ingredients in a small bowl.
2. Use immediately.

Paprika-Oregano Seasoning

Prep time: 5 minutes | Cook time: 0 minutes | Makes about ¾ cups

- 3 tablespoons ancho chile powder
- 3 tablespoons paprika
- 2 tablespoons dried oregano
- 2 tablespoons freshly ground black pepper
- 2 teaspoons cayenne
- 2 teaspoons cumin
- 1 tablespoon granulated onion
- 1 tablespoon granulated garlic

1. Stir together all the ingredients in a small bowl.
2. Use immediately or place in an airtight container in the pantry.

Ginger-Garlic Dipping Sauce

Prep time: 15 minutes | Cook time: 0 minutes | Makes about 1 cup

- ¼ cup rice vinegar
- ¼ cup hoisin sauce
- ¼ cup low-sodium chicken or vegetable stock
- 3 tablespoons soy sauce
- 1 tablespoon minced or grated ginger
- 1 tablespoon minced or pressed garlic
- 1 teaspoon chili-garlic sauce or sriracha (or more to taste)

1. Stir together all the ingredients in a small bowl, or place in a jar with a tight-fitting lid and shake until well mixed.
2. Use immediately.

Creamy Corn Meal

Prep time: 3 minutes | Cook time: 1 hour 5 minutes | Makes about 4 cups

- 1 cup corn meal or polenta (not instant or quick cook)
- 2 cups chicken or vegetable stock
- 2 cups milk
- 2 tablespoons unsalted butter, cut into 4 pieces
- 1 teaspoon flake salt or ½ teaspoon fine salt

1. Add the corn meal to the baking pan. Stir in the stock, milk, butter, and salt.
2. Select Bake. set temperature to 160°C and set time to 1 hour and 5 minutes. Press Start to begin preheating.
3. Once the unit has preheated, place the pan into the Air Fryer.
4. After 15 minutes, remove the pan from the Air Fryer and stir the polenta. Return the pan to the Air Fryer and continue cooking.
5. After 30 minutes, remove the pan again and stir the polenta again. Return the pan to the Air Fryer and continue cooking for 15 to 20 minutes, or until the polenta is soft and creamy and the liquid is absorbed.
6. When done, remove the pan from the Air Fryer.
7. Serve immediately.

Poblano Garlic Sauce

Prep time: 15 minutes | Cook time: 0 minutes | Makes 2 cups

- 3 large ancho chiles, stems and seeds removed, torn into pieces
- 1½ cups very hot water
- 2 garlic cloves, peeled and lightly smashed
- 2 tablespoons wine vinegar
- 1½ teaspoons sugar
- ½ teaspoon dried oregano
- ½ teaspoon ground cumin
- 2 teaspoons flake salt or 1 teaspoon fine salt

1. Mix together the chile pieces and hot water in a bowl and let stand for 10 to 15 minutes.
2. Pour the chiles and water into a blender jar. Fold in the garlic, vinegar, sugar, oregano, cumin, and salt and blend until smooth.
3. Use immediately.

Baked White Rice

Prep time: 3 minutes | Cook time: 35 minutes | Makes about 4 cups

- 1 cup long-grain white rice, rinsed and drained
- 1 tablespoon unsalted butter, melted, or 1 tablespoon extra-virgin olive oil
- 2 cups water
- 1 teaspoon flake salt or ½ teaspoon fine salt

1. Add the butter and rice to the baking pan and stir to coat. Pour in the water and sprinkle with the salt. Stir until the salt is dissolved.
2. Select Bake. Set temperature to 160°C and set time to 35 minutes. Press Start to begin preheating.
3. Once the unit has preheated, place the pan into the Air Fryer.
4. After 20 minutes, remove the pan from the Air Fryer. Stir the rice. Transfer the pan back to the Air Fryer and continue cooking for 10 to 15 minutes, or until the rice is mostly cooked through and the water is absorbed.
5. When done, remove the pan from the Air Fryer and cover with tin foil . Let stand for 10 minutes. Using a fork, gently fluff the rice.
6. Serve immediately.

Hemp Dressing

Prep time: 5 minutes | Cook time: 0 minutes | Makes 2 cups

- ½ cup white wine vinegar
- ¼ cup tahini
- ¼ cup water
- 1 tablespoon hemp seeds
- ½ tablespoon freshly squeezed lemon juice
- 1 teaspoon garlic powder
- 1 teaspoon dried oregano
- 1 teaspoon dried basil
- 1 teaspoon red pepper flakes
- ½ teaspoon onion powder
- ½ teaspoon pink Himalayan salt
- ½ teaspoon freshly ground black pepper

1. In a bowl, combine all the ingredients and whisk until mixed well.

©SpendWithPennies.com

Garlic Lime Tahini Dressing

Prep time: 5 minutes | Cook time: 0 minutes | Makes about ¾ cup

- ⅓ cup tahini
- 3 tablespoons filtered water
- 2 tablespoons freshly squeezed lime juice
- 1 tablespoon apple cider vinegar
- 1 teaspoon lime zest
- 1½ teaspoons raw honey
- ¼ teaspoon garlic powder
- ¼ teaspoon salt

1. Whisk together the tahini, water, vinegar, lime juice, lime zest, honey, salt, and garlic powder in a small bowl until well emulsified.
2. Serve immediately, or refrigerate in an airtight container for to 1 week.

Red Enchilada Sauce

Prep time: 15 minutes | Cook time: 0 minutes | Makes 2 cups

- 3 large ancho chiles, stems and seeds removed, torn into pieces
- 1½ cups very hot water
- 2 garlic cloves, peeled and lightly smashed
- 2 tablespoons wine vinegar
- 2 teaspoons flaked salt or 1 teaspoon fine salt
- 1½ teaspoons sugar
- ½ teaspoon dried oregano
- ½ teaspoon ground cumin

1. Mix together the chile pieces and hot water in a bowl and let stand for 10 to 15 minutes.
2. Pour the chiles and water into a blender jar. Fold in the garlic, vinegar, salt, sugar, oregano, and cumin, and salt and blend until smooth.
3. Use immediately.

Avocado Dressing

Prep time: 5 minutes | Cook time: 0 minutes | Makes 2 cups

- 1 large avocado, pitted and peeled
- ½ cup water
- 2 tablespoons tahini
- 2 tablespoons freshly squeezed lemon juice
- 1 teaspoon dried basil
- 1 teaspoon white wine vinegar
- 1 garlic clove
- ¼ teaspoon pink Himalayan salt
- ¼ teaspoon freshly ground black pepper

1. Combine all the ingredients in a food processor and blend until smooth.

Fresh Mixed Berry Vinaigrette

Prep time: 15 minutes | Cook time: 0 minutes | Makes about 1½ cups

- 1 cup mixed berries, thawed if frozen
- ½ cup balsamic vinegar
- ⅓ cup extra-virgin olive oil
- 2 tablespoons freshly squeezed lemon or lime juice
- 1 tablespoon lemon or lime zest
- 1 tablespoon Dijon mustard
- 1 tablespoon raw honey or maple syrup
- 1 teaspoon salt
- ½ teaspoon freshly ground black pepper

1. Place all the ingredients in a blender and purée until thoroughly mixed and smooth.
2. You can serve it over a bed of greens, grilled meat, or fresh fruit salad.

Lemon Dijon Vinaigrette

Prep time: 5 minutes | Cook time: 0 minutes | Makes about 6 tablespoons

- ¼ cup extra-virgin olive oil
- 1 garlic clove, minced
- 2 tablespoons freshly squeezed lemon juice
- 1 teaspoon Dijon mustard
- ½ teaspoon raw honey
- ¼ teaspoon salt
- ¼ teaspoon dried basil

1. Place all the ingredients in a mason jar. Cover and shake vigorously until thoroughly mixed and well emulsified.
2. Serve chilled.

Chapter 3
Breakfasts

Sweet Banana Bread
Prep time: 10 minutes | Cook time: 40 minutes | Serves 6

- 2 ripe bananas
- 1 egg
- ½ cup skim milk
- 2 tablespoons honey
- 1 tablespoon vegetable oil
- 1 cup unbleached flour
- ¾ cup chopped trail mix
- 1 teaspoon baking powder
- Salt, to taste

1. Process the bananas, egg, milk, honey, and oil in a blender or food processor until smooth and transfer to a mixing bowl.
2. Add the flour and trail mix, stirring to mix well. Add the baking powder and stir just enough to blend it into the batter. Add salt, to taste. Pour the mixture into an oiled or nonstick loaf pan.
3. Select Bake. Set temperature to 200°C and set time to 40 minutes. Select Start to begin preheating.
4. Once preheated, slide the pan into the Air Fryer.
5. When done, a toothpick inserted in the center will come out clean.
6. Serve.

Ranch Risotto with Parmesan Cheese
Prep time: 10 minutes | Cook time: 30 minutes | Serves 2

- 1 tablespoon olive oil
- 1 clove garlic, minced
- 1 tablespoon unsalted butter
- 1 onion, diced
- ¾ cup Arborio rice
- 2 cups chicken stock, boiling
- ½ cup Parmesan cheese, grated

1. Select the BAKE function and preheat Air Fryer to 200°C.
2. Grease a round baking tin with olive oil and stir in the garlic, butter, and onion.
3. Transfer the tin to the air fryer oven and bake for 4 minutes. Add the rice and bake for 4 more minutes.
4. Turn the air fryer oven to 160°C and pour in the chicken stock. Cover and bake for 22 minutes. Scatter with cheese and serve.

Cheesy Italian banger Egg Muffins

Prep time: 5 minutes | Cook time: 20 minutes | Serves 4

- 6 ounces (170 g) Italian banger, sliced
- 6 eggs
- ⅛ cup double cream
- Salt and ground black pepper, to taste
- 3 ounces (85 g) Parmesan cheese, grated
- Cooking spray

1. Select the BAKE function and preheat Air Fryer to 180°C.
2. Spritz a muffin pan with cooking spray. Put the sliced banger in the muffin pan.
3. Beat the eggs with the cream in a bowl and season with salt and pepper.
4. Pour half of the mixture over the bangers in the pan.
5. Sprinkle with cheese and the remaining egg mixture.
6. Bake in the preheated air fryer oven for 20 minutes or until set.
7. Serve immediately.

Simple Blueberry Muffins

Prep time: 10 minutes | Cook time: 12 minutes | Makes 8 muffins

- 1⅓ cups flour
- ½ cup sugar
- 2 teaspoons baking powder
- ¼ teaspoon salt
- ⅓ cup rapeseed oil
- 1 egg
- ½ cup milk
- ⅔ cup blueberries, fresh or frozen and thawed

1. Select the BAKE function and preheat Air Fryer to 170°C.
2. In a medium bowl, stir together flour, sugar, baking powder, and salt. In a separate bowl, combine oil, egg, and milk and mix well.
3. Add egg mixture to dry ingredients and stir just until moistened. Gently stir in the blueberries.
4. Spoon batter evenly into greaseproof paper-lined muffin cups. Put 4 muffin cups in air fryer basket or wire rack and bake for 12 minutes or until tops spring back when touched lightly.
5. Repeat with the remaining muffins.
6. Serve immediately.

Easy Cinnamon Toasts

Prep time: 5 minutes | Cook time: 4 minutes | Serves 4

- 1 tablespoon salted butter
- 2 teaspoons ground cinnamon
- 4 tablespoons sugar
- ½ teaspoon vanilla extract
- 10 bread slices

1. Select the BAKE function and preheat Air Fryer to 190°C.
2. In a bowl, combine the butter, cinnamon, sugar, and vanilla extract.
3. Spread onto the slices of bread.
4. Put the bread inside the air fryer oven and bake for 4 minutes or until golden brown.
5. Serve warm.

Mozzarella Pepperoni Pizza

Prep time: 10 minutes | Cook time: 6 minutes | Serves 1

- 1 teaspoon olive oil
- 1 tablespoon pizza sauce
- 1 pita bread
- 6 pepperoni slices
- ¼ cup grated Mozzarella cheese
- ¼ teaspoon garlic powder
- ¼ teaspoon dried oregano

1. Select the BAKE function and preheat Air Fryer to 180°C.
2. Grease the air fryer basket or wire rack with olive oil.
3. Spread the pizza sauce on top of the pita bread.
4. Put the pepperoni slices over the sauce, followed by the Mozzarella cheese. Season with garlic powder and oregano.
5. Put the pita pizza inside the air fryer oven and place a trivet on top.
6. Bake in the preheated air fryer oven for 6 minutes and serve.

Scotch Eggs

Prep time: 5 minutes | Cook time: 25 minutes | Serves 4

- 4 large hard boiled eggs
- 1 (12-ounce / 340-g) package pork banger
- 8 slices thick-cut bacon

SPECIAL EQUIPMENT:
- 4 wooden Cocktail Sticks, soaked in water for at least 30 minutes

1. Slice the banger into four parts and place each part into a large circle.
2. Put an egg into each circle and wrap it in the banger.
3. Put in the refrigerator for 1 hour. Make a cross with two pieces of thick-cut bacon.
4. Put a wrapped egg in the center, fold the bacon over top of the egg, and secure with a toothpick.
5. Select the AIR FRY function and cook at 200°C for 25 minutes.
6. Serve immediately.

Warm Sourdough Croutons

Prep time: 5 minutes | Cook time: 6 minutes | Makes 4 cups

- 4 cups cubed sourdough bread, 1-inch cubes
- 1 tablespoon olive oil
- 1 teaspoon fresh thyme leaves
- ¼ teaspoon salt
- Freshly ground black pepper, to taste

1. Combine all ingredients in a bowl.
2. Toss the bread cubes into the air fryer oven.
3. Select the AIR FRY function and cook at 200°C for 6 minutes, shaking the air fryer basket or wire rack once or twice while they cook.
4. Serve warm.

Ricotta Spinach Omelet

Prep time: 10 minutes | Cook time: 10 minutes | Serves 1

- 1 teaspoon olive oil
- 3 eggs
- Salt and ground black pepper, to taste
- 1 tablespoon ricotta cheese
- ¼ cup chopped spinach
- 1 tablespoon chopped parsley

1. Grease the air fryer basket or wire rack with olive oil.
2. Select the BAKE function and preheat Air Fryer to 170°C.
3. In a bowl, beat the eggs with a fork and sprinkle salt and pepper.
4. Add the ricotta, spinach, and parsley and then transfer to the air fryer oven.
5. Bake for 10 minutes or until the egg is set.
6. Serve warm.

Spinach and Tomato with Scrambled Eggs

Prep time: 10 minutes | Cook time: 10 minutes | Serves 2

- 2 tablespoons olive oil
- 4 eggs, whisked
- 5 ounces (142 g) fresh spinach, chopped
- 1 medium tomato, chopped
- 1 teaspoon fresh lemon juice
- ½ teaspoon coarse salt
- ½ teaspoon ground black pepper
- ½ cup of fresh basil, roughly chopped

1. Grease a baking pan with the oil, tilting it to spread the oil around.
2. Select the BAKE function and preheat Air Fryer to 280°F (138°C).
3. Mix the remaining ingredients, apart from the basil leaves, whisking well until everything is completely combined.
4. Bake in the air fryer oven for 10 minutes.
5. Top with fresh basil leaves before serving.

Lime-Honey Grilled Fruit Salad

Prep time: 5 minutes | Cook time: 4 minutes | Serves 4

- ½ pound (227 g) strawberries, washed, hulled and halved
- 1 (9-ounce / 255-g) can pineapple chunks, drained, juice reserved
- 2 peaches, pitted and sliced
- 6 tablespoons honey, divided
- 1 tablespoon freshly squeezed lime juice

1. Insert the Grill Grate and close the hood. Select GRILL, set the temperature to MAX, and set the time to 4 minutes. Select START/STOP to begin preheating.
2. While the unit is preheating, combine the strawberries, pineapple, and peaches in a large bowl with 3 tablespoons of honey. Toss to coat evenly.
3. When the unit beeps to signify it has preheated, place the fruit on the Grill Grate. Gently press the fruit down to maximize grill marks. Close the hood and grill for 4 minutes without flipping.
4. Meanwhile, in a small bowl, combine the remaining 3 tablespoons of honey, lime juice, and 1 tablespoon of reserved pineapple juice.
5. When cooking is complete, place the fruit in a large bowl and toss with the honey mixture. Serve immediately.

Stuffed Bell Pepper with Cheddar Bacon

Prep time: 10 minutes | Cook time: 10 minutes | Serves 4

- 1 cup shredded Cheddar cheese
- 4 slices bacon, cooked and chopped
- 4 bell peppers, seeded and tops removed
- 4 large eggs
- Sea salt, to taste
- Freshly ground black pepper, to taste
- Chopped fresh parsley, for garnish

1. Insert the Crisper Basket and close the hood. Select AIR CRISP, set the temperature to 200°C, and set the time to 15 minutes. Select START/STOP to begin preheating.
2. Meanwhile, divide the cheese and bacon between the bell peppers. Crack one of the eggs into each bell pepper, and season with salt and pepper.
3. When the unit beeps to signify it has preheated, place each bell pepper in the air fryer basket or wire rack. Close the hood and cook for 10 to 15 minutes, until the egg whites are cooked and the yolks are slightly runny.
4. Remove the peppers from the air fryer basket or wire rack, garnish with parsley, and serve.

Glazed Strawberry Toast

Prep time: 5 minutes | Cook time: 8 minutes | Makes 4 toasts

- 4 slices bread, ½-inch thick
- 1 cup sliced strawberries
- 1 teaspoon sugar
- Cooking spray

1. On a clean work surface, lay the bread slices and spritz one side of each slice of bread with cooking spray.
2. Place the bread slices in the air fryer basket or wire rack, sprayed side down. Top with the strawberries and a sprinkle of sugar.
3. Select Air Fry, set temperature to 190°C, and set time to 8 minutes. Select Start/Stop to begin preheating.
4. Once preheated, place the air fryer basket or wire rack on the air fry position.
5. When cooking is complete, the toast should be well browned on each side. Remove from the Air Fryer to a plate and serve.

Egg in a Hole

Prep time: 5 minutes | Cook time: 5 minutes | Serves 1

- 1 slice bread
- 1 teaspoon butter, softened
- 1 egg
- Salt and pepper, to taste
- 1 tablespoon shredded Cheddar cheese
- 2 teaspoons diced ham

1. On a flat work surface, cut a hole in the center of the bread slice with a 2½-inch-diameter biscuit cutter.
2. Spread the butter evenly on each side of the bread slice and transfer to a baking dish.
3. Crack the egg into the hole and season as desired with salt and pepper. Scatter the shredded cheese and diced ham on top.
4. Select Bake, set temperature to 170°C, and set time to 5 minutes. Select Start/Stop to begin preheating.
5. Once preheated, place the baking dish on the bake position.
6. When cooking is complete, the bread should be lightly browned and the egg should be set. Remove from the Air Fryer and serve hot.

Bacon and Egg Stuffed Peppers

Prep time: 10 minutes | Cook time: 15 minutes | Serves 4

- 1 cup shredded Cheddar cheese
- 4 slices bacon, cooked and chopped
- 4 bell peppers, seeded and tops removed
- 4 large eggs
- Sea salt, to taste
- Freshly ground black pepper, to taste
- Chopped fresh parsley, for garnish

1. Place the crisper tray on the air fry position. Select Air Fry, set the temperature to 200°C, and set the time to 15 minutes.
2. Meanwhile, divide the cheese and bacon between the bell peppers. Crack one of the eggs into each bell pepper, and season with salt and pepper.
3. Place each bell pepper in the crisper tray. Air fry for 10 to 15 minutes, until the egg whites are cooked and the yolks are slightly runny.
4. Remove the peppers from the crisper tray, garnish with parsley, and serve.

Grit and Ham Fritters

Prep time: 15 minutes | Cook time: 20 minutes | Serves 6 to 8

- 4 cups water
- 1 cup quick-cooking corn meal
- ¼ teaspoon salt
- 2 tablespoons butter
- 2 cups grated Cheddar cheese, divided
- 1 cup finely diced ham
- 1 tablespoon chopped chives
- Salt and freshly ground black pepper, to taste
- 1 egg, beaten
- 2 cups panko bread crumbs
- Cooking spray

1. Bring the water to a boil in a saucepan. Whisk in the corn meal and ¼ teaspoon of salt, and cook for 7 minutes until the corn meal are soft. Remove the pan from the heat and stir in the butter and 1 cup of the grated Cheddar cheese. Transfer the corn meal to a bowl and let them cool for 10 to 15 minutes.
2. Stir the ham, chives and the rest of the cheese into the corn meal and season with salt and pepper to taste. Add the beaten egg and refrigerate the mixture for 30 minutes.
3. Put the panko bread crumbs in a shallow dish. Measure out ¼-cup portions of the corn meal mixture and shape them into patties. Coat all sides of the patties with the panko bread crumbs, patting them with the hands so the crumbs adhere to the patties. You should have about 16 patties. Spritz both sides of the patties with cooking spray.
4. Preheat the air fryer to 200°C.
5. In batches of 5 or 6, air fry the fritters for 8 minutes. Using a flat spatula, flip the fritters over and air fry for another 4 minutes.
6. Serve hot.

Ham and Corn Muffins

Prep time: 10 minutes | Cook time: 6 minutes | Makes 8 muffins

- ¾ cup yellow cornmeal
- ¼ cup flour
- 1½ teaspoons baking powder
- ¼ teaspoon salt
- 1 egg, beaten
- 2 tablespoons rapeseed oil
- ½ cup milk
- ½ cup shredded sharp Cheddar cheese
- ½ cup diced ham

1. Preheat the air fryer to 200°C.
2. In a medium bowl, stir together the cornmeal, flour, baking powder, and salt.
3. Add the egg, oil, and milk to dry ingredients and mix well.
4. Stir in shredded cheese and diced ham.
5. Divide batter among 8 parchment-paper-lined muffin cups.
6. Put 4 filled muffin cups in air fryer basket or wire rack and bake for 5 minutes.
7. Reduce temperature to 170°C and bake for 1 minute or until a toothpick inserted in center of the muffin comes out clean.
8. Repeat steps 6 and 7 to bake remaining muffins.
9. Serve warm.

Chocolate Chips Honey Muffins

Prep time: 5 minutes | Cook time: 15 minutes | Serves 6

- ½ cup plain flour
- ⅓ cup almond flour
- 1 teaspoon baking powder
- A pinch of sea salt
- A pinch of grated nutmeg
- 1 egg
- ¼ cup honey
- ¼ cup milk
- 1 teaspoon vanilla extract
- 4 tablespoons coconut oil
- ½ cup dark chocolate chips

1. Mix all ingredients in a bowl. Scrape the batter into silicone baking molds; place them in the baking dish.
2. Place the baking dish in the air fryer basket or wire rack. and bake in the preheated instant pot at 160°C for 15 minutes or until a tester comes out dry and clean.
3. Allow the muffins to cool before unmolding and serving. Bon appétit!

Buttery Banana Muffins

Prep time: 10 minutes | Cook time: 15 minutes | Serves 4

- 1 large egg, whisked
- 1 ripe banana, peeled and mashed
- ¼ cup butter, melted
- ¼ cup Maple Syrup
- ½ cup plain flour
- ¼ almond flour
- 1 teaspoon baking powder
- ¼ cup Demerara sugar
- ½ teaspoon vanilla essence
- 1 teaspoon cinnamon powder
- ¼ teaspoon ground cloves

1. Mix all ingredients in a bowl.
2. Scrape the batter into silicone baking molds; place them in the baking dish.
3. Place the baking dish in the air fryer basket or wire rack. and bake in the preheated instant pot at 160°C for 15 minutes or until a tester comes out dry and clean.
4. Allow the muffins to cool before unmolding and serving.

Chapter 4
Fish and Seafood

Roasted Salmon with Vegetables

Prep time: 15 minutes | Cook time: 14 minutes | Serves 2

- 1 large carrot, peeled and sliced
- 1 fennel bulb, thinly sliced
- 1 small onion, thinly sliced
- ¼ cup low-fat Soured cream
- 2 (5-ounce / 142-g) salmon fillets

FROM THE CUPBOARD:

- ¼ teaspoon coarsely ground pepper

1. Preheat the Duo Crisp to 200°C.
2. In a bowl, mix together the carrot, fennel bulb, and onion. Toss well.
3. Transfer the vegetable mixture to a 6-inch metal pan, then put the pan in the Duo Crisp basket.
4. Roast in the preheated air fryer for 4 minutes, or until the vegetables are fork-tender.
5. Remove the pan from the Duo Crisp. Add the Soured cream to the pan and season with ground pepper, then spread the salmon fillets on top.
6. Return the pan to the Duo Crisp and roast for an additional 10 minutes, or until the fish flakes easily when tested with a fork.
7. Let the salmon and vegetables cool for 5 minutes before serving.

Roasted Salmon Croquettes

Prep time: 5 minutes | Cook time: 15 minutes | Serves 6

- 1 (14.75-ounce / 418-g) can Alaskan pink salmon, drained and bones removed
- 1 egg, whisked
- ½ cup bread crumbs
- 1 teaspoon garlic powder
- 2 scallions, diced

FROM THE CUPBOARD:

- Cooking spray
- Salt and pepper, to taste

1. Preheat the Duo Crisp to 200°C.
2. Add the salmon, whisked egg, bread crumbs, garlic powder, scallions, salt, and pepper to a large bowl. Stir to combine well.
3. Make the salmon croquettes: Scoop out the salmon mixture and shape into 6 equal-sized patties with your hands.
4. Put the patties in the Duo Crisp basket and spray with cooking spray.
5. Roast in the preheated air fryer for 7 minutes. Flip the patties and cook for 3 to 4 minutes more, or until the patties are golden brown.
6. Remove the salmon croquettes from the air fryer basket or wire rack and serve.

Quick Coconut Prawn

Prep time: 10 minutes | Cook time: 8 minutes | Serves 4

- ¼ cup plain flour
- 1 egg
- ⅓ cup shredded unsweetened coconut
- ¼ cup panko bread crumbs
- 1 pound (454 g) raw Prawn, peeled, deveined and patted dry

FROM THE CUPBOARD:

- Cooking spray
- Salt and pepper, to taste

1. Preheat the Duo Crisp to 200°C.
2. On a plate, place the flour. In a small bowl, whisk the egg until frothy. In a separate bowl, mix together the coconut, bread crumbs, salt, and pepper.
3. Dredge the Prawn in the flour, shaking off any excess, then dip them in the egg, and finally coat them in the coconut-bread mixture.
4. Spritz the Duo Crisp basket with cooking spray. Put the breaded Prawn in the air fryer basket or wire rack and spray with cooking spray.
5. Cook in the preheated air fryer for 8 minutes, flipping the Prawn once during cooking, or until the Prawn are opaque and crisp.
6. Remove from the air fryer basket or wire rack and serve on a plate.

Lemon-Pepper Tilapia Fillets

Prep time: 5 minutes | Cook time: 15 minutes | Serves 4

- 4 tilapia fillets
- 1 teaspoon garlic powder
- 1 teaspoon paprika
- 1 teaspoon dried basil
- Lemon-pepper seasoning, to taste

FROM THE CUPBOARD:

- 1 tablespoon extra-virgin olive oil

1. Preheat the Duo Crisp to 200°C.
2. Add the olive oil, garlic powder, paprika, basil, lemon-pepper seasoning, and fillets to a large bowl, and toss well to coat the fillets thoroughly.
3. Transfer the coated fillets to the Duo Crisp basket.
4. Cook in the preheated air fryer for 8 minutes. Flip the fillets and cook for 7 minutes more until the fish flakes easily with a fork.
5. Divide the fillets among four serving plates and serve hot.

Blackened Prawn with Lemon Juice

Prep time: 5 minutes | Cook time: 10 minutes | Serves 4

- 1 pound (454 g) raw Prawn, peeled, deveined and patted dry
- 1 teaspoon paprika
- ½ teaspoon cayenne pepper
- ½ teaspoon dried oregano
- Juice of ½ lemon

FROM THE CUPBOARD:

- Cooking spray
- Salt and pepper, to taste

1. Preheat the Duo Crisp to 200°C.
2. Put the Prawn in a sealable plastic bag. Add the paprika, cayenne pepper, oregano, lemon juice, salt, and pepper to the Prawn. Seal the bag and shake to evenly coat the Prawn with the spices.
3. Spritz the Duo Crisp basket with cooking spray. Arrange the Prawn in the air fryer basket or wire rack.
4. Cook in the preheated air fryer for 7 minutes, shaking the air fryer basket or wire rack once during cooking, or until the Prawn is blackened.
5. Let the Prawn cool for 5 minutes and serve warm.

Fried Catfish with Fish Fry

Prep time: 5 minutes | Cook time: 13 minutes | Serves 4

- 4 catfish fillets, rinsed and patted dry
- ¼ cup seasoned fish fry
- 1 tablespoon chopped parsley

FROM THE CUPBOARD:

- 1 tablespoon olive oil

1. Preheat the Duo Crisp to 200°C.
2. Place the fillets and seasoned fish fry in a Ziploc bag. Seal the bag and shake well until the fish is nicely coated.
3. Brush both sides of each piece of fish with olive oil. Place the fillets in the Duo Crisp basket.
4. Cook in the preheated air fryer for 13 minutes, flip the fillets once during cooking, or until the fish is cooked through.
5. Remove from the air fryer basket or wire rack and garnish with chopped parsley.

Pecan-Crusted Catfish Fillets

Prep time: 5 minutes | Cook time: 12 minutes | Serves 4

- ½ cup pecan meal
- 4 (4-ounce / 113-g) catfish fillets, rinsed and patted dry
- Fresh oregano, for garnish (optional)
- Pecan halves, for garnish (optional)

FROM THE CUPBOARD:

- 1 tablespoon avocado oil, divided
- 1 teaspoon fine sea salt
- ¼ teaspoon ground black pepper

1. Preheat the Duo Crisp to 190°C. Grease the Duo Crisp basket with half of the avocado oil and set aside.
2. Stir together the pecan meal, salt, and pepper in a large bowl. Roll the fillets with the mixture, pressing so the fish is well coated.
3. Brush the fillets with the remaining avocado oil and transfer to the Duo Crisp basket.
4. Cook in the preheated air fryer for 12 minutes, flipping the fillets halfway through, or until the fish flakes easily with a fork.
5. Remove from the air fryer basket or wire rack to a large plate. Sprinkle the oregano and pecan halves on top for garnish, if desired.

Fish Fillets with Parmesan Cheese

Prep time: 5 minutes | Cook time: 10 to 12 minutes | Serves 4

- 1 cup Parmesan cheese, grated
- 1 egg, whisked
- 1 teaspoon garlic powder
- ½ teaspoon shallot powder
- 4 white fish fillets

FROM THE CUPBOARD:

- Salt and ground black pepper, to taste

1. Preheat the Duo Crisp to 190°C.
2. In a shallow dish, put the Parmesan cheese. Mix together the whisked egg, garlic powder, and shallot powder in a bowl, and stir to combine.
3. On a clean work surface, season the fillets generously with salt and pepper. Dredge the fillets into the egg mixture, then roll over the cheese until thickly coated.
4. Arrange the fillets in the Duo Crisp basket and air fry until golden brown, about 10 to 12 minutes.
5. Let the fish fillets cool for 5 minutes before serving.

Air-Fried Sardinas

Prep time: 10 minutes | Cook time: 12 minutes | Serves 4

- 1½ pounds (680 g) Sardines, rinsed and patted dry
- 1 tablespoon lemon juice
- 1 tablespoon Italian seasoning mix

FROM THE CUPBOARD:

- 2 tablespoons olive oil
- 1 tablespoon soy sauce
- Salt and ground black pepper, to taste

1. Preheat the Duo Crisp to 180°C.
2. In a large bowl, toss the Sardines with the olive oil, lemon juice, Italian seasoning mix, soy sauce, salt, and pepper. Let the Sardines marinate for 30 minutes.
3. Put the marinated Sardines in the Duo Crisp basket and air fry for about 12 minutes until flaky, flipping the fish halfway through.
4. Transfer to a plate and serve hot.

Garlicky Prawn

Prep time: 5 minutes | Cook time: 3 to 4 minutes | Serves 4

- 1½ pounds (680 g) Prawn, shelled and deveined
- 3 cloves garlic, minced
- 1 teaspoon smoked cayenne pepper
- ½ teaspoon ginger, freshly grated
- ½ tablespoon fresh basil leaves, chopped

FROM THE CUPBOARD:

- 1½ tablespoons olive oil
- 1 teaspoon sea salt

1. Preheat the Duo Crisp to 200°C.
2. Mix together all the ingredients in a large bowl and toss until well incorporated. Let the Prawn sit for 30 minutes.
3. Place the Prawn in the Duo Crisp basket and air fry for 3 to 4 minutes, or until the Prawn are opaque. Serve hot.

Tuna Steaks with Red Onions

Prep time: 10 minutes | Cook time: 10 minutes | Serves 4

- 4 tuna steaks
- ½ pound (227 g) red onions
- 1 teaspoon dried rosemary
- 1 tablespoon cayenne pepper
- 1 lemon, sliced

FROM THE CUPBOARD:

- Cooking spray
- 4 teaspoons olive oil
- ½ teaspoon sea salt
- ½ teaspoon black pepper

1. Preheat the Duo Crisp to 200°C and spray the air fryer basket or wire rack with cooking spray.
2. Place the tuna steaks in the air fryer basket or wire rack and scatter the onions all over. Drizzle with the olive oil and sprinkle with rosemary, cayenne pepper, salt, and black pepper.
3. Bake in batches in the preheated air fryer for 10 minutes until cooked through.
4. Garnish with the lemon slices and serve warm.

Parmesan Haddock Fillets

Prep time: 5 minutes | Cook time: 11 to 13 minutes | Serves 2

- ½ cup Parmesan cheese, freshly grated
- 1 teaspoon dried parsley flakes
- 1 egg
- ¼ teaspoon cayenne pepper
- 2 haddock fillets, patted dry

FROM THE CUPBOARD:

- 2 tablespoons olive oil
- ½ teaspoon coarse sea salt
- ¼ teaspoon ground black pepper

1. Preheat the Duo Crisp to 180°C.
2. Stir together the Parmesan cheese and parsley flakes in a shallow dish. Beat the egg with the cayenne pepper, sea salt, and pepper in a bowl.
3. Dunk the haddock fillets into the egg, and then roll over the Parmesan mixture until fully coated on both sides.
4. Transfer the fillets to the Duo Crisp basket and drizzle with the olive oil.
5. Cook in the preheated air fryer for 11 to 13 minutes, or until the flesh is opaque.
6. Remove from the air fryer basket or wire rack to a plate and serve.

Crispy Catfish Strips

Prep time: 5 minutes | Cook time: 16 to 18 minutes | Serves 4

- 1 cup buttermilk
- 5 catfish fillets, cut into 1½-inch strips
- Cooking spray
- 1 cup cornmeal
- 1 tablespoon Cajun, Cajun, or Old Bay seasoning

1. Pour the buttermilk into a shallow baking pan. Place the catfish in the dish and refrigerate for at least 1 hour to help remove any fishy taste.
2. Place the crisper tray on the air fry position. Select Air Fry, set the temperature to 200°C, and set the time to 18 minutes.
3. Spray the crisper tray lightly with cooking spray.
4. In a shallow bowl, combine cornmeal and Cajun seasoning.
5. Shake any excess buttermilk off the catfish. Place each strip in the cornmeal mixture and coat completely. Press the cornmeal into the catfish gently to help it stick.
6. Place the strips in the crisper tray in a single layer. Lightly spray the catfish with cooking spray. You may need to cook the catfish in more than one batch.
7. Air fry for 8 minutes. Turn the catfish strips over and lightly spray with cooking spray. air fry until golden brown and crispy, for 8 to 10 more minutes.
8. Serve warm.

Simple Salmon Patty Bites

Prep time: 15 minutes | Cook time: 10 to 15 minutes | Serves 4

- 4 (5-ounce / 142-g) cans pink salmon, skinless, boneless in water, drained
- 2 eggs, beaten
- 1 cup whole-wheat panko bread crumbs
- 4 tablespoons finely minced red bell pepper
- 2 tablespoons parsley flakes
- 2 teaspoons Old Bay seasoning
- Cooking spray

1. Place the crisper tray on the air fry position. Select Air Fry, set the temperature to 180°C , and set the time to 15 minutes.
2. Spray the crisper tray lightly with cooking spray.
3. In a medium bowl, mix the salmon, eggs, panko bread crumbs, red bell pepper, parsley flakes, and Old Bay seasoning.
4. Using a small biscuit scoop, form the mixture into 20 balls.
5. Place the salmon bites in the crisper tray in a single layer and spray lightly with cooking spray. You may need to cook them in batches.
6. Air fry for 10 to 15 minutes until crispy, shaking the crisper tray a couple of times for even cooking.
7. Serve immediately.

Crispy Cod Cakes with Salad Greens

Prep time: 15 minutes | Cook time: 12 minutes | Serves 4

- 1 pound (454 g) cod fillets, cut into chunks
- ⅓ cup packed fresh basil leaves
- 3 cloves garlic, crushed
- ½ teaspoon smoked paprika
- ¼ teaspoon salt
- ¼ teaspoon pepper
- 1 large egg, beaten
- 1 cup panko bread crumbs
- Cooking spray
- Salad greens, for serving

1. In a food processor, pulse cod, basil, garlic, smoked paprika, salt, and pepper until cod is finely chopped, stirring occasionally. Form into 8 patties, about 2 inches in diameter. Dip each first into the egg, then into the panko, patting to adhere. Spray with oil on one side.
2. Place the crisper tray on the air fry position. Select Air Fry, set the temperature to 200°C, and set the time to 12 minutes.
3. Working in batches, place half the cakes in the crisper tray, oil-side down; spray with oil. Air fry for 12 minutes, until golden brown and cooked through.
4. Serve cod cakes with salad greens.

Roasted Cod with Sesame Seeds

Prep time: 5 minutes | Cook time: 7 to 9 minutes | Makes 1 fillet

- 1 tablespoon reduced-sodium soy sauce
- 2 teaspoons honey
- Cooking spray
- 6 ounces (170 g) fresh cod fillet
- 1 teaspoon sesame seeds

1. Place the crisper tray on the roast position. Select Roast, set the temperature to 180°C , and set the time to 10 minutes.
2. In a small bowl, combine the soy sauce and honey.
3. Spray the crisper tray with cooking spray, then place the cod in the crisper tray, brush with the soy mixture, and sprinkle sesame seeds on top.
4. Roast for 7 to 9 minutes, or until opaque.
5. Remove the fish and allow to cool on a wire rack for 5 minutes before serving.

Cajun-Style Salmon Burgers

Prep time: 10 minutes | Cook time: 10 to 15 minutes | Serves 4

- 4 (5-ounce / 142-g) cans pink salmon in water, any skin and bones removed, drained
- 2 eggs, beaten
- 1 cup whole-wheat bread crumbs
- 4 tablespoons light mayonnaise
- 2 teaspoons Cajun seasoning
- 2 teaspoons dry mustard
- 4 whole-wheat buns
- Cooking spray

1. In a medium bowl, mix the salmon, egg, bread crumbs, mayonnaise, Cajun seasoning, and dry mustard. Cover with Cling Film and refrigerate for 30 minutes.
2. Place the crisper tray on the air fry position. Select Air Fry, set the temperature to 180°C , and set the time to 15 minutes.
3. Spray the crisper tray lightly with cooking spray.
4. Shape the mixture into four ½-inch-thick patties about the same size as the buns.
5. Place the salmon patties in the crisper tray in a single layer and lightly spray the tops with cooking spray. You may need to cook them in batches.
6. Air fry for 6 to 8 minutes. Turn the patties over and lightly spray with cooking spray. air fry until crispy on the outside, for 4 to 7 more minutes.
7. Serve on whole-wheat buns.

Goat Cheese Prawn

Prep time: 15 minutes | Cook time: 7 to 8 minutes | Serves 2

- 1 pound (454 g) Prawn, deveined
- 1½ tablespoons olive oil
- 1½ tablespoons balsamic vinegar
- 1 tablespoon coconut aminos
- ½ tablespoon fresh parsley, roughly chopped
- Sea salt flakes, to taste
- 1 teaspoon Dijon mustard
- ½ teaspoon smoked cayenne pepper
- ½ teaspoon garlic powder
- Salt and ground black peppercorns, to taste
- 1 cup shredded goat cheese

1. Place the crisper tray on the air fry position. Select Air Fry, set the temperature to 200°C, and set the time to 8 minutes.
2. Except for the cheese, stir together all the ingredients in a large bowl until the Prawn are evenly coated.
3. Arrange the Prawn in the crisper tray. Air fry for 7 to 8 minutes, shaking the crisper tray halfway through, or until the Prawn are pink and cooked through.
4. Serve the Prawn with the shredded goat cheese sprinkled on top.

Chapter 5
Meats

Beef Brisket with BBQ Sauce

Prep time: 5 minutes | Cook time: 1 hour | Serves 4

- 1½ pounds (680 g) beef brisket
- ¼ cup barbecue sauce
- 2 tablespoons soy sauce

1. Start by preheating the air fryer to 200°C.
2. Toss the beef with the remaining ingredients; place the beef in the crisper tray.
3. Place the crisper tray in the corresponding position in the air fryer. Select Roast and cook the beef for 15 minutes, turn the beef over and reduce the temperature to 180°C .
4. Continue to cook the beef for 55 minutes more. Bon appétit!

Beef Roast with Carrot

Prep time: 10 minutes | Cook time: 55 minutes | Serves 5

- 2 pounds (907 g) top sirloin roast
- 2 tablespoons olive oil
- Sea salt and ground black pepper, to taste
- 2 carrots, sliced
- 1 tablespoon fresh coriander
- 1 tablespoon fresh thyme
- 1 tablespoon fresh rosemary

1. Start by preheating the air fryer to 200°C.
2. Toss the beef with the olive oil, salt, and black pepper; place the beef in the crisper tray.
3. Place the crisper tray in the corresponding position in the air fryer. Select Roast and cook the beef for 45 minutes, turning it over halfway through the cooking time.
4. Top the beef with the carrots and herbs. Continue to cook an additional 10 minutes.
5. Enjoy!

Air Fried Beef Ribs

Prep time: 20 minutes | Cook time: 8 minutes | Serves 4

- 1 pound (454 g) meaty beef ribs, rinsed and drained
- 3 tablespoons apple cider vinegar
- 1 cup coriander, finely chopped
- 1 tablespoon fresh basil leaves, chopped
- 2 garlic cloves, finely chopped
- 1 chipotle powder
- 1 teaspoon fennel seeds
- 1 teaspoon hot paprika
- flake salt and black pepper, to taste
- ½ cup vegetable oil

1. Coat the ribs with the remaining ingredients and refrigerate for at least 3 hours.
2. Preheat the air fryer oven to 180°C .
3. Separate the ribs from the marinade and put them in the air fryer basket or wire rack.
4. Place the air fryer basket or wire rack onto the baking pan and slide into Rack Position 2, select Air Fry and set time to 8 minutes.
5. Pour the remaining marinade over the ribs and serve.

Butter London Broil

Prep time: 5 minutes | Cook time: 28 minutes | Serves 4

- 1½ pounds (680 g) London broil
- flake salt and ground black pepper, to taste
- ¼ teaspoon ground bay leaf
- 3 tablespoons butter
- 1 tablespoon Dijon mustard
- 1 teaspoon crushed garlic
- 1 tablespoon chopped fresh parsley

1. Start by preheating the air fryer to 200°C.
2. Toss the beef with the salt and black pepper; place the beef in a lightly oiled crisper tray.
3. Place the crisper tray in the corresponding position in the air fryer. Select Roast and cook the beef for 28 minutes, turning over halfway through the cooking time.
4. In the meantime, mix the butter with the remaining ingredients and place it in the refrigerator until well chilled.
5. Serve warm beef with the chilled garlic butter on the side. Bon appétit!

Beef Brisket Carnitas
Prep time: 5 minutes | Cook time: 1 hour | Serves 4

- 1½ pounds (680 g) beef brisket
- 2 tablespoons olive oil
- Sea salt and ground black pepper, to taste
- 1 teaspoon chili powder
- 4 medium-sized flour tortillas

1. Start by preheating the air fryer to 200°C.
2. Toss the beef brisket with the olive oil, salt, black pepper, and chili powder; now, place the beef brisket in the crisper tray.
3. Place the crisper tray in the corresponding position in the air fryer. Select Roast and cook the beef brisket for 15 minutes, turn the beef over and reduce the temperature to 180°C .
4. Continue to cook the beef brisket for approximately 55 minutes or until cooked through.
5. Shred the beef with two forks and serve with tortillas and toppings of choice. Bon appétit!

Flank Steak with Paprika
Prep time: 5 minutes | Cook time: 12 minutes | Serves 5

- 2 pounds (907 g) flank steak
- 2 tablespoons olive oil
- 1 teaspoon paprika
- Sea salt and ground black pepper, to taste

1. Start by preheating the air fryer to 200°C.
2. Toss the steak with the remaining ingredients; place the steak in the crisper tray.
3. Place the crisper tray in the corresponding position in the air fryer. Select Air Fry and cook the steak for 12 minutes, turning over halfway through the cooking time.
4. Bon appétit!

Spicy Beef Meatloaf

Prep time: 10 minutes | Cook time: 25 minutes | Serves 4

- 1½ pounds (680 g) ground chuck
- ½ onion, chopped
- 1 teaspoon minced habanero pepper
- ¼ cup crushed tortilla chips
- 1 teaspoon minced garlic
- Sea salt and ground black pepper, to taste
- 2 tablespoons olive oil
- 1 egg, whisked

1. Start by preheating the air fryer to 200°C.
2. Thoroughly combine all ingredients until everything is well combined.
3. Scrape the beef mixture into a lightly oiled baking pan.
4. Place the baking pan in the corresponding position in the air fryer. Select Bake and cook the meatloaf for 25 minutes. Bon appétit!

Filet Mignon with Basil

Prep time: 5 minutes | Cook time: 14 minutes | Serves 4

- 1½ pounds (680 g) filet mignon
- Sea salt and ground black pepper, to taste
- 2 tablespoons olive oil
- 1 teaspoon dried rosemary
- 1 teaspoon dried thyme
- 1 teaspoon dried basil
- 2 cloves garlic, minced

1. Start by preheating the air fryer to 200°C.
2. Toss the beef with the remaining ingredients; place the beef in the crisper tray.
3. Place the crisper tray in the corresponding position in the air fryer. Select Air Fry and cook the beef for 14 minutes, turning it over halfway through the cooking time.
4. Enjoy!

Beef Cheese Muffins

Prep time: 10 minutes | Cook time: 25 minutes | Serves 4

MEATLOAVES:

- 1 pound (454 g) minced beef
- ¼ cup seasoned bread crumbs
- ¼ cup grated Parmesan cheese
- 1 small onion, minced
- 2 garlic cloves, pressed
- 1 egg, beaten
- Sea salt and ground black pepper, to taste

GLAZE:

- 4 tablespoons tomato sauce
- 1 tablespoon Demerara sugar
- 1 tablespoon Dijon mustard

1. Start by preheating the air fryer to 190°C.
2. Thoroughly combine all ingredients for the meatloaves until everything is well combined.
3. Scrape the beef mixture into lightly oiled silicone cups and transfer them to the baking pan.
4. Place the baking pan in the corresponding position in the air fryer. Select Bake and cook the beef cups for 20 minutes.
5. In the meantime, mix the remaining ingredients for the glaze. Then, spread the glaze on top of each muffin; continue to cook for another 5 minutes.
6. Bon appétit!

Ribeye Steak with Cheese

Prep time: 5 minutes | Cook time: 15 minutes | Serves 4

- 1 pound (454 g) ribeye steak, bone-in
- Sea salt and ground black pepper, to taste
- 2 tablespoons olive oil
- ½ teaspoon onion powder
- 1 teaspoon garlic powder
- 1 cup crumbled blue cheese

1. Start by preheating the air fryer to 200°C.
2. Toss the ribeye steak with the salt, black pepper, olive oil, onion powder, and garlic powder; place the ribeye steak in the crisper tray.
3. Place the crisper tray in the corresponding position in the air fryer. Select Air Fry and cook the ribeye steak for 15 minutes, turning it over halfway through the cooking time.
4. Top the ribeye steak with the cheese and serve warm. Bon appétit!

Rump Roast with Paprika

Prep time: 5 minutes | Cook time: 50 minutes | Serves 4

- 1½ pounds (680 g) rump roast
- Ground black pepper and flaked salt, to taste
- 1 teaspoon paprika
- 2 tablespoons olive oil
- ¼ cup brandy
- 2 tablespoons cold butter

1. Start by preheating the air fryer to 200°C.
2. Toss the rump roast with the black pepper, salt, paprika, olive oil, and brandy; place the rump roast in a lightly oiled crisper tray.
3. Place the crisper tray in the corresponding position in the air fryer. Select Roast and cook for 50 minutes, turning it over halfway through the cooking time.
4. Serve with the cold butter and enjoy!

Coulotte Roast with Garlic

Prep time: 10 minutes | Cook time: 55 minutes | Serves 5

- 2 pounds (907 g) Coulotte roast
- 2 tablespoons olive oil
- 1 tablespoon finely chopped fresh parsley
- 1 tablespoon finely chopped fresh Coriander
- 2 garlic cloves, minced
- flake salt and ground black pepper, to taste

1. Start by preheating the air fryer to 200°C.
2. Toss the roast beef with the remaining ingredients; place the roast beef in the crisper tray.
3. Place the crisper tray in the corresponding position in the air fryer. Select Roast and cook for 55 minutes, turning over halfway through the cooking time.
4. Enjoy!

Garlicky Beef Tenderloin

Prep time: 10 minutes | Cook time: 20 minutes | Serves 4

- 1½ pounds (680 g) beef tenderloin, sliced
- 2 tablespoons sesame oil
- 1 teaspoon five-spice powder
- 2 garlic cloves, minced
- 1 teaspoon peeled and grated fresh ginger
- 2 tablespoons soy sauce

1. Start by preheating the air fryer to 200°C.
2. Toss the beef tenderloin with the remaining ingredients; place the beef tenderloin in the crisper tray.
3. Place the crisper tray in the corresponding position in the air fryer. Select Air Fry and cook the beef tenderloin for 20 minutes, turning it over halfway through the cooking time.
4. Enjoy!

Beef Steaks with Fish Sauce

Prep time: 5 minutes | Cook time: 14 minutes | Serves 4

- 1½ pounds (680 g) Tomahawk steaks
- 2 bell peppers, sliced
- 2 tablespoons butter, melted
- 2 teaspoons steak seasoning
- 2 tablespoons fish sauce
- Sea salt and ground black pepper, to taste

1. Start by preheating the air fryer to 200°C.
2. Toss all ingredients in the crisper tray.
3. Place the crisper tray in the corresponding position in the air fryer. Select Air Fry and cook the steak and peppers for about 14 minutes, turning it over halfway through the cooking time.
4. Bon appétit!

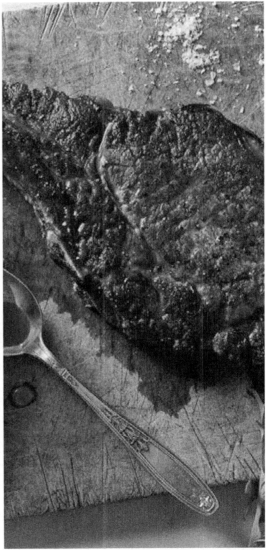

Mushroom and Beef Patties Rolls

Prep time: 5 minutes | Cook time: 15 minutes | Serves 4

- 1 pound (454 g) ground chuck
- 2 garlic cloves, minced
- 1 small onion, chopped
- 1 cup chopped mushrooms
- 1 teaspoon cayenne pepper
- Sea salt and ground black pepper, to taste
- 4 brioche rolls

1. Start by preheating the air fryer to 190°C.
2. Mix the ground chuck, garlic, onion, mushrooms, cayenne pepper, salt, and black pepper until everything is well combined. Form the mixture into four patties.
3. Arrange the patties in the crisper tray.
4. Place the crisper tray in the corresponding position in the air fryer. Select Air Fry and cook the patties for about 15 minutes or until cooked through; make sure to turn them over halfway through the cooking time.
5. Serve the patties on the prepared brioche rolls and enjoy!

Lamb Koftas

Prep time: 15 minutes | Cook time: 8 minutes | Serves 3 to 4

- 1 pound (454 g) ground lamb
- 1 egg, beaten
- 1 teaspoon ground coriander
- 1 teaspoon ground cumin
- 2 tablespoons chopped fresh mint
- ½ teaspoon salt
- Freshly ground black pepper, to taste

SPECIAL EQUIPMENT:
- 5 wooden skewers, soaked for at least 30 minutes

1. Preheat the air fryer to 200°C. Spritz the air fryer basket or wire rack with cooking spray.
2. Put all the ingredients in a bowl. Stir to mix well. Then divide and shape the mixture into 10 ovals.
3. Snap the skewers in half and run the skewers through each lamb oval to make the koftas
4. Arrange the koftas in the preheated air fryer and cook for 8 minutes or until well browned on both sides. Flip the koftas halfway through the cooking time.
5. Remove the koftas from the air fryer and serve warm.

Air Fried Lamb Steaks and Red Potatoes

Prep time: 10 minutes | Cook time: 15 minutes | Serves 2

- 2 lamb steaks
- 2 red potatoes, sliced
- 2 garlic cloves, crushed
- 2 tablespoons fresh thyme, chopped
- Salt and ground black pepper, to taste

1. Preheat the air fryer to 180°C . Spritz the air fryer basket or wire rack with cooking spray.
2. Arrange the lamb steaks and potatoes in the air fryer basket or wire rack and sprinkle with crushed garlic, salt, and black pepper.
3. Cook in the preheated air fryer for 14 to 16 minutes or until the lamb steaks are well browned. Flip the lamb steaks and potatoes with tongs halfway through the cooking time.
4. Serve them immediately on a platter with thyme on top.

Herbed Lamb Chops with Roasted Garlic

Prep time: 5 minutes | Cook time: 25 minutes | Serves 4

- 1 garlic head, halved lengthwise
- ½ tablespoon thyme
- ½ tablespoon oregano
- 4 lamb chops
- 1 tablespoons olive oil
- Salt and ground black pepper, to taste

1. Preheat the air fryer to 200°C. Spritz the air fryer basket or wire rack with cooking spray.
2. Roast the garlic in the greased air fryer basket or wire rack for 10 minutes until the garlic head is soft.
3. Meanwhile, combine the thyme, oregano, olive oil, salt, and black pepper in a bowl.
4. Remove the garlic from the air fryer basket or wire rack and allow to cool for a few minutes. Squeeze the roasted garlic in the herb mixture. Stir to mix well.
5. Dunk the lamb chops in the bowl of mixture to coat well. Then Place the lamb chops in the air fryer basket or wire rack.
6. Cook for 12 minutes or until the lamb chops are well browned. Flip the lamb chops with tongs halfway through the cooking time.
7. Serve the lamb chops immediately.

Red Curry Steak

Prep time: 6 hours to 8 hours | Cook time: 12 to 18 minutes | Serves 4

- 3 tablespoons red curry paste
- 2 teaspoons fresh ginger, grated
- 3 scallions, minced
- 1½ pounds (680 g) flank steak
- Fresh Coriander leaves, for garnish
- ¼ cup olive oil
- 2 tablespoons soy sauce
- 2 tablespoons rice wine vinegar
- Salt and ground black pepper, to taste

1. Combine the red curry paste, ginger, soy sauce, rice vinegar, scallions, and olive oil in a bowl.
2. Put the flank steak on a large plate, then pierce with a skewer as many times as possible. Baste half of the paste mixture over the steak. Flip the steak and repeat the instructions above.
3. Wrap the plate in plastic and refrigerate to marinate for 6 to 8 hours.
4. Remove the marinated steak from the refrigerator and let stand for 30 minutes.
5. Meanwhile, preheat the air fryer to 200°C.
6. Arrange the steak in the air fryer basket or wire rack and baste with marinade. Sprinkle with salt and black pepper.
7. Cook for 12 to 18 minutes or until the flank steak reaches your desired doneness. Flip the steak halfway through the cooking time.
8. Remove the steak from the air fryer and slice to serve.

Air Fried Pork Tenderloin with Godlen Apples

Prep time: 10 minutes | Cook time: 30 minutes | Serves 2 to 3

1 (1-pound / 454-g) pork tenderloin
2 tablespoons coarse brown mustard
1½ teaspoons finely chopped fresh rosemary, plus sprigs for garnish
2 apples, cored and cut into 8 wedges
Salt and ground black pepper, to taste
1 teaspoon Demerara sugar
1 tablespoon butter, melted

1. Preheat the air fryer to 190°C. Spritz the air fryer basket or wire rack with cooking spray.
2. On a clean work surface, brush the pork tenderloin with brown mustard, then sprinkle with rosemary, salt, and black pepper.
3. Place the pork tenderloin in the air fryer basket or wire rack and cook for 15 to 18 minutes or until an instant-read thermometer inserted in the thickest part of the pork tenderloin registers at least 60°C. Flip the pork tenderloin halfway through the cooking time.
4. Meanwhile, combine the Demerara sugar and butter in a bowl, then put the apple wedges in the mixture and toss to coat well.
5. Remove the pork tenderloin from the air fryer basket or wire rack and increase the temperature of the air fryer to 200°C.
6. Cook the apple in the air fryer basket or wire rack for 8 minutes or until the apples are golden brown. Shake the air fryer basket or wire rack twice during the cooking.
7. Transfer the pork tenderloin and apples onto a large plate and spread the rosemary sprigs before serving.

Chapter 6
Poultry

Soy Sauce Duck Fillet

Prep time: 5 minutes | Cook time: 30 minutes | Serves 4

- 1½ pounds (680 g) duck fillet
- 1 tablespoon honey
- 2 tablespoons dark soy sauce
- 1 tablespoon soybean paste

1. Start by preheating the air fryer to 170°C.
2. Toss the duck fillet with the remaining ingredients. Place the duck fillet in the baking pan.
3. Place the baking pan in the corresponding position in the air fryer. Select Bake and cook the duck fillet for 15 minutes, turning them over halfway through the cooking time.
4. Increase the temperature to 180°C and continue to cook for about 15 minutes or until cooked through.
5. Let it rest for 10 minutes before carving and serving. Bon appétit!

Chicken Patties with Chili Sauce

Prep time: 5 minutes | Cook time: 17 minutes | Serves 4

- 1 pound (454 g) ground chicken
- 1 tablespoon olive oil
- 1 small onion, chopped
- 1 teaspoon minced garlic
- 1 tablespoon chili sauce
- flake salt and ground black pepper, to taste

1. Start by preheating the air fryer to 190°C.
2. Mix all ingredients until everything is well combined. Form the mixture into four patties.
3. Arrange the patties in the crisper tray.
4. Place the crisper tray in the corresponding position in the air fryer. Select Air Fry and cook the patties for about 17 minutes or until cooked through; make sure to turn them over halfway through the cooking time.
5. Bon appétit!

Chicken Cheese Muffins

Prep time: 5 minutes | Cook time: 12 minutes | Serves 4

- 1 pound (454 g) chicken breasts
- 1 tablespoon olive oil
- Sea salt and black pepper, to taste
- 4 slices Cheddar cheese
- 4 teaspoons yellow mustard
- 4 English muffins, lightly toasted

1. Start by preheating the air fryer to 190°C.
2. Pat the chicken dry with kitchen towels. Toss the chicken breasts with the olive oil, salt, and pepper. Place the chicken in the crisper tray.
3. Place the crisper tray in the corresponding position in the air fryer. Select Roast and cook the chicken for 12 minutes, turning them over halfway through the cooking time.
4. Shred the chicken using two forks and serve with cheese, mustard, and English muffins. Bon appétit!

Bacon and Cheese Stuffed Chicken

Prep time: 5 minutes | Cook time: 20 minutes | Serves 4

- 1 pound (454 g) chicken breasts
- 4 tablespoons goat cheese
- 4 tablespoons bacon
- 1 tablespoon olive oil
- ½ teaspoon garlic powder
- 1 teaspoon dried basil
- 1 teaspoon dried oregano
- 1 teaspoon dried parsley flakes

1. Start by preheating the air fryer to 200°C.
2. Flatten the chicken breasts with a mallet.
3. Stuff each piece of chicken with cheese and bacon. Roll them up and secure with Cocktail Sticks.
4. Then, sprinkle the chicken with olive oil, garlic powder, basil, oregano, and parsley.
5. Place the stuffed chicken breasts in the crisper tray. Place the crisper tray in the corresponding position in the air fryer. Select Air Fry and cook the chicken for about 20 minutes, turning them over halfway through the cooking time.
6. Bon appétit!

Panko Chicken with Olives
Prep time: 10 minutes | Cook time: 12 minutes | Serves 4

- 1 pound (454 g) chicken fillets, boneless, skinless
- 2 eggs, whisked
- 1 teaspoon dried basil
- ½ teaspoon dried rosemary
- ½ teaspoon dried oregano
- ½ teaspoon crushed red pepper flakes
- ½ cup seasoned bread crumbs
- 2 ounces (57 g) Kalamata olives, pitted and sliced

1. Start by preheating the air fryer to 190°C.
2. Pat the chicken dry with kitchen paper.
3. In a shallow bowl, thoroughly combine the eggs and spices. Place the bread crumbs in a separate shallow bowl.
4. Dip the chicken fillets into the egg mixture. Then, roll the chicken fillets over the bread crumbs. Arrange the chicken fillets in the crisper tray.
5. Place the crisper tray in the corresponding position in the air fryer. Select Air Fry and cook the chicken fillets for 12 minutes, turning them over halfway through the cooking time.
6. Serve with Kalamata olives and enjoy!

Chicken Drumsticks
Prep time: 5 minutes | Cook time: 22 minutes | Serves 3

- 3 chicken drumsticks
- 2 tablespoons sesame oil
- flake salt and ground black pepper, to taste
- 1 tablespoon soy sauce
- 1 teaspoon five-spice powder

1. Start by preheating the air fryer to 190°C.
2. Pat the chicken drumsticks dry with kitchen paper. Toss the chicken drumsticks with the remaining ingredients. Place the chicken drumsticks in the crisper tray.
3. Place the crisper tray in the corresponding position in the air fryer. Select Roast and cook the chicken drumsticks for 22 minutes, turning them over halfway through the cooking time.
4. Bon appétit!

Chicken Drumsticks with chili sauce

Prep time: 5 minutes | Cook time: 20 minutes | Serves 4

- ½ cup plain flour
- 1 tablespoon Ranch seasoning mix
- 1 pound (454 g) chicken drumsticks
- 1 tablespoon chili sauce
- Sea salt and ground black pepper, to taste

1. Start by preheating the air fryer to 190°C.
2. Pat the chicken drumsticks dry with kitchen paper. Toss the chicken drumsticks with the remaining ingredients. Arrange the chicken drumsticks in the crisper tray.
3. Place the crisper tray in the corresponding position in the air fryer. Select Air Fry and cook the chicken drumsticks for 20 minutes, turning them over halfway through the cooking time.
4. Bon appétit!

Duck with Miso Paste

Prep time: 5 minutes | Cook time: 30 minutes | Serves 5

- 2 pounds (907 g) duck breasts
- 1 tablespoon butter, melted
- 2 tablespoons Cranberry Juice
- 2 tablespoons miso paste
- 1 teaspoon minced garlic
- 1 teaspoon peeled and minced ginger
- 1 teaspoon five-spice powder

1. Start by preheating the air fryer to 170°C.
2. Pat the duck breasts dry with kitchen paper. Toss the duck breasts with the remaining ingredients. Place the duck breasts in the baking pan.
3. Place the baking pan in the corresponding position in the air fryer. Select Bake and cook the duck breasts for 15 minutes, turning them over halfway through the cooking time.
4. Increase the temperature to 180°C and continue to cook for about 15 minutes or until cooked through.
5. Let it rest for 10 minutes before carving and serving. Bon appétit!

Chicken Fillets with Cheese

Prep time: 5 minutes | Cook time: 12 minutes | Serves 4

- 1½ pounds (680 g) chicken fillets
- 2 tablespoons olive oil
- 1 teaspoon smoked paprika
- 1 teaspoon Italian seasoning mix
- Sea salt and ground black pepper, to taste
- ½ cup grated Pecorino Romano cheese

1. Start by preheating the air fryer to 190°C.
2. Pat the chicken fillets dry with kitchen paper. Toss the chicken fillets with the olive oil and spices. Place the chicken fillets in the crisper tray.
3. Place the crisper tray in the corresponding position in the air fryer. Select Air Fry and cook the chicken fillets for 12 minutes, turning them over halfway through the cooking time.
4. Top the chicken fillets with grated cheese and serve warm. Bon appétit!

Baked Turkey Cheese Taquitos

Prep time: 5 minutes | Cook time: 24 minutes | Serves 6

- 1 pound (454 g) turkey breasts, boneless and skinless
- flake salt and freshly ground black pepper, to taste
- 1 clove garlic, minced
- 1 habanero pepper, minced
- 4 ounces (113 g) Mexican cheese blend, shredded
- 6 small corn tortillas
- ½ cup salsa

1. Start by preheating the air fryer to 190°C.
2. Pat the turkey breasts dry with kitchen towels. Toss the turkey breasts with the salt and black pepper. Arrange the turkey breasts in the crisper tray.
3. Place the crisper tray in the corresponding position in the air fryer. Select Air Fry and cook the turkey breasts for 18 minutes, turning them over halfway through the cooking time.
4. Place the shredded chicken, garlic, habanero pepper, and cheese on one end of each tortilla. Roll them up tightly and transfer them to a lightly oiled baking pan.
5. Reduce the temperature to 180°C . Place the baking pan in the corresponding position in the air fryer. Select Bake and cook the taquitos for 6 minutes. Serve the taquitos with salsa and enjoy!

Chicken Cheese Tortilla

Prep time: 8 minutes | Cook time: 12 minutes | Serves 4

- 1 egg, whisked
- ½ cup grated Parmesan cheese
- ½ cup crushed tortilla chips
- ½ teaspoon onion powder
- ½ teaspoon garlic powder
- 1 teaspoon red chili powder
- 1½ pounds (680 g) chicken breasts, boneless, skinless, cut into strips

1. Start by preheating the air fryer to 190°C.
2. Whisk the egg in a shallow bowl. In a separate bowl, whisk the Parmesan cheese, tortilla chips, onion powder, garlic powder, and red chili powder.
3. Dip the chicken pieces into the egg mixture. Then, roll the chicken pieces over the bread crumb mixture. Place the chicken in the crisper tray.
4. Place the crisper tray in the corresponding position in the air fryer. Select Air Fry and cook the chicken for 12 minutes, turning them over halfway through the cooking time.
5. Bon appétit!

Fried Buffalo Chicken Taquitos

Prep time: 15 minutes | Cook time: 5 to 10 minutes | Serves 6

- 8 ounces (227 g) fat-free cream cheese, softened
- ⅛ cup Buffalo sauce
- 2 cups shredded cooked chicken
- 12 (7-inch) low-carb flour tortillas
- Olive oil spray

1. Preheat the air fryer oven to 180°C . Spray the air fryer basket or wire rack lightly with olive oil spray.
2. In a large bowl, mix together the cream cheese and Buffalo sauce until well combined. Add the chicken and stir until combined.
3. Place the tortillas on a clean workspace. Spoon 2 to 3 tablespoons of the chicken mixture in a thin line down the center of each tortilla. Roll up the tortillas.
4. Place the tortillas in the air fryer basket or wire rack, seam-side down. Spray each tortilla lightly with olive oil spray. You may need to cook the taquitos in batches.
5. Air fry until golden brown, 5 to 10 minutes. Serve hot.

Crispy Chicken Strips

Prep time: 15 minutes | Cook time: 20 minutes | Serves 4

- 1 tablespoon olive oil
- 1 pound (454 g) boneless, skinless chicken tenderloins
- 1 teaspoon salt
- ½ teaspoon freshly ground black pepper
- ½ teaspoon paprika
- ½ teaspoon garlic powder
- ½ cup whole-wheat seasoned bread crumbs
- 1 teaspoon dried parsley
- Cooking spray

1. Preheat the air fryer oven to 190°C. Spray the air fryer basket or wire rack lightly with cooking spray.
2. In a medium bowl, toss the chicken with the salt, pepper, paprika, and garlic powder until evenly coated.
3. Add the olive oil and toss to coat the chicken evenly.
4. In a separate, shallow bowl, mix together the bread crumbs and parsley.
5. Coat each piece of chicken evenly in the bread crumb mixture.
6. Place the chicken in the air fryer basket or wire rack in a single layer and spray it lightly with cooking spray. You may need to cook them in batches.
7. Air fry for 10 minutes. Flip the chicken over, lightly spray it with cooking spray, and air fry for an additional 8 to 10 minutes, until golden brown. Serve.

Fajita Chicken Strips

Prep time: 10 minutes | Cook time: 15 minutes | Serves 4

- 1 pound (454 g) boneless, skinless chicken tenderloins, cut into strips
- 3 bell peppers, any colour, cut into chunks
- 1 onion, cut into chunks
- 1 tablespoon olive oil
- 1 tablespoon fajita seasoning mix
- Cooking spray

1. Preheat the air fryer oven to 190°C.
2. In a large bowl, mix together the chicken, bell peppers, onion, olive oil, and fajita seasoning mix until completely coated.
3. Spray the air fryer basket or wire rack lightly with cooking spray.
4. Place the chicken and vegetables in the air fryer basket or wire rack and lightly spray with cooking spray.
5. Air fry for 7 minutes. Shake the air fryer basket or wire rack and air fry for an additional 5 to 8 minutes, until the chicken is cooked through and the veggies are starting to char.
6. Serve warm.

Lemon Parmesan Chicken

Prep time: 10 minutes | Cook time: 20 minutes | Serves 4

- 1 egg
- 2 tablespoons lemon juice
- 2 teaspoons minced garlic
- ½ teaspoon salt
- ½ teaspoon freshly ground black pepper
- 4 boneless, skinless chicken breasts, thin cut
- Olive oil spray
- ½ cup whole-wheat bread crumbs
- ¼ cup grated Parmesan cheese

1. In a medium bowl, whisk together the egg, lemon juice, garlic, salt, and pepper. Add the chicken breasts, cover, and refrigerate for up to 1 hour.
2. In a shallow bowl, combine the bread crumbs and Parmesan cheese.
3. Preheat the air fryer oven to 180°C . Spray the air fryer basket or wire rack lightly with olive oil spray.
4. Remove the chicken breasts from the egg mixture, then dredge them in the bread crumb mixture, and place in the air fryer basket or wire rack in a single layer. Lightly spray the chicken breasts with olive oil spray. You may need to cook the chicken in batches.
5. Air fry for 8 minutes. Flip the chicken over, lightly spray with olive oil spray, and air fry until the chicken reaches an internal temperature of 75°C, for an additional 7 to 12 minutes.
6. Serve warm.

Sweet-and-Sour Drumsticks

Prep time: 5 minutes | Cook time: 23 to 25 minutes | Serves 4

- 6 chicken drumsticks
- 3 tablespoons lemon juice, divided
- 3 tablespoons low-sodium soy sauce, divided
- 1 tablespoon groundnut oil
- 3 tablespoons honey
- 3 tablespoons Demerara sugar
- 2 tablespoons ketchup
- ¼ cup pineapple juice

1. Preheat the air fryer oven to 180°C.
2. Sprinkle the drumsticks with 1 tablespoon of lemon juice and 1 tablespoon of soy sauce. Place in the air fryer basket or wire rack and drizzle with the groundnut oil. Toss to coat. Select Bake with Convection, and cook for 18 minutes or until the chicken is almost done.
3. Meanwhile, in a metal bowl, combine the remaining 2 tablespoons of lemon juice, the remaining 2 tablespoons of soy sauce, honey, Demerara sugar, ketchup, and pineapple juice.
4. Add the cooked chicken to the bowl and stir to coat the chicken well with the sauce.
5. Place the metal bowl in the air fryer basket or wire rack. Select Bake with Convection, and cook for 5 to 7 minutes or until the chicken is glazed and registers 75°C on a meat thermometer. Serve warm.

Fry Balsamic Chicken Strips

Prep time: 10 minutes | Cook time: 18 minutes | Serves 4

- 1 pound (454 g) chicken breasts, cut into strips
- 2 tomatoes, cubed
- 1 green chili pepper, cut into stripes
- ½ teaspoon cumin
- 2 spring onions, sliced
- 2 tablespoon olive oil
- 1 tablespoon yellow mustard
- ½ teaspoon ginger powder
- 2 tablespoon fresh Coriander, chopped
- Salt and black pepper to taste

1. Heat olive oil in a deep pan over medium heat and sauté mustard, spring onions, ginger powder, cumin, and green chili pepper for 2 to 3 minutes.
2. Stir in tomatoes, Coriander, and salt; set aside. Preheat the air fryer to 190°C. Season the chicken with salt and pepper, and place in the greased air fryer basket or wire rack.
3. Air Fry for 15 minutes, shaking once. Top with the sauce and serve.

Sesame Chicken with Sweet Wasabi

Prep time: 5 minutes | Cook time: 16 minutes | Serves 2

- 2 tablespoon wasabi
- 1 tablespoon agave syrup
- 2 teaspoon black sesame seeds
- Salt and black pepper to taste
- 2 chicken breasts, cut into large chunks

1. In a bowl, mix wasabi, agave syrup, sesame seed, salt, and pepper. Rub the mixture onto the breasts.
2. Arrange the breasts on a greased frying basket and cook for 16 minutes, turning once halfway through.

Crunchy Coconut Chicken with Berry Sauce

Prep time: 5 minutes | Cook time: 16 minutes | Serves 4

- 2 cups coconut flakes
- 4 chicken breasts, cut into strips
- ½ cup cornflour
- Salt and black pepper to taste
- 2 eggs, beaten

1. Preheat air fryer to 180°C. Mix salt, pepper, and cornflour in a bowl. Line a frying basket with greaseproof paper.
2. Dip the chicken first in the cornflour, then into the eggs, and finally, coat with coconut flakes.
3. Arrange in the air fryer and Bake for 16 minutes, flipping once until crispy. Serve with berry sauce.

Turmeric Chicken Fillets with Sweet Chili

Prep time: 5 minutes | Cook time: 18 minutes | Serves 4

- 2 chicken breasts, halved
- Salt and black pepper to taste
- ¼ cup sweet chili sauce
- 1 teaspoon taste

1. Preheat air fryer to 200°C. In a bowl, add salt, black pepper, sweet chili sauce, and turmeric; mix well.
2. Lightly brush the chicken with the mixture and place it in the frying basket. Air Fry for 12 to 14 minutes, turning once halfway through. Serve with a side of steamed greens.

Avocado and Mango Chicken Breasts

Prep time: 10 minutes | Cook time: 14 minutes | Serves 2

- 2 chicken breasts
- 1 mango, chopped
- 1 avocado, sliced
- 1 red pepper, chopped
- 1 tablespoon balsamic vinegar
- 2 tablespoon olive oil
- 2 garlic cloves, minced
- ½ teaspoon dried oregano
- 1 teaspoon mustard powder
- Salt and black pepper to taste

1. In a bowl, mix garlic, olive oil, and balsamic vinegar. Add in the breasts, cover, and marinate for 2 hours.
2. Preheat the fryer to 180°C. Place the chicken in the frying basket and Air Fry for 12 to 14 minutes, flipping once.
3. Top with avocado, mango, and red pepper. Drizzle with balsamic vinegar and serve.

Chapter 7
Veggies and Fruits

Sweet Cinnamon Pineapple Slices

Prep time: 5 minutes | Cook time: 12 hours | Serves 6

- 1 pineapple, peeled, cored and sliced ¼ inch thick
- 1 tablespoon coconut palm sugar
- 2 teaspoons ground cinnamon
- ½ teaspoon ground ginger
- ½ teaspoon Himalayan pink salt

1. Toss the pineapple slices with the sugar, cinnamon, ginger and salt.
2. Place the pineapple slices in a single layer on three air flow racks. Place the racks on the bottom, middle, and top shelves of the air fryer oven.
3. Press the Power Button. Cook at 120°F (49°C) for 12 hours.

Citrusy Strawberry Splenda Fruit Mixture

Prep time: 5 minutes | Cook time: 9 hours | Serves 2

- 2 cups fresh strawberries
- 3 tablespoons Splenda
- ½ lemon, juiced

1. Blend your strawberries, sugar and lemon juice until smooth.
2. Line the air flow racks with greaseproof paper.
3. Spread the fruit mixture evenly across the racks.
4. Slide the racks into the air fryer oven. Press the Power Button. Cook at 140°F (60°C) for 9 hours, or until it is no longer sticky.
5. Cut into slices and roll.
6. Store in an air tight container at room temperature for up to a month or in the freezer for up to a year.

Air Fried Strawberry Slices

Prep time: 5 minutes | Cook time: 2 hours | Serves 4

- 1 pound (454 g) fresh strawberries

1. Line three air flow racks with greaseproof paper.
2. Wash strawberries and cut off stem ends. Cut strawberries into slices, about ⅛ inch thick.
3. Place sliced strawberries on the air flow racks. Space them so the pieces are not touching.
4. Slide the racks into the air fryer oven. Press the Power Button. Cook at 170°F (77°C) for 30 minutes. Use tongs to turn the berries. Cook for another 30 minutes. Repeat this until strawberry slices are leathery.
5. Allow the slices to cool completely. Transfer dried strawberry slices to an airtight container. They will keep up to 5 days.

Homemade Fruit Leather

Prep time: 5 minutes | Cook time: 6 hours 15 minutes | Serves 4

- 4 peaches, pitted and each peach cut into 6 pieces

1. Line three air flow racks with greaseproof paper. Place peach slices on parchment.
2. Slide the racks into the air fryer oven. Press the Power Button. Cook at 200°C for 15 minutes.
3. Transfer the cooked peaches to a blender or food processor and blend until smooth.
4. Line a baking tray with greaseproof paper and pour peach purée onto paper, spreading as necessary with a spatula into an even layer.
5. Slide the sheet into the air fryer oven. Press the Power Button. Cook at 130°F (54°C) for 6 hours or until leather is desired consistency.

Air Fried Mushrooms

Prep time: 5 minutes | Cook time: 4 hours | Makes 2½ quarts

- 4 to 5 pounds (1.8 to 2.3 kg) fresh mushrooms, washed, rinsed and drained well.

1. Rinse whole mushrooms well under cold running water. Gently scrub any visible dirt away without damaging the mushroom. Pat dry with kitchen paper if needed.
2. Break the stem off of each mushroom and slice into ¼ to ½ inch thick slices with a sharp knife.
3. Place the sliced mushrooms on the parchment-lined air flow racks.
4. Slide the racks into the air fryer oven. Press the Power Button. Cook at 170°F (77°C) for 4 hours.
5. Check the mushrooms after 1 hour and flip them over for even drying. Check the mushroom slices every hour.
6. As the mushroom slices dry, remove them from the air fryer oven and allow cooling on the racks or a paper towel.
7. Store dried mushroom slices in an airtight glass container.

Air Fred courgette Chips

Prep time: 5 minutes | Cook time: 3 hours | Serves 4

- 4 to 5 medium courgette, thinly sliced
- 2 tablespoons olive oil
- Garlic salt and black pepper, to taste

1. Toss the courgette with the olive oil, garlic salt and pepper.
2. Lay in a single layer on the air flow racks. Slide the racks into the air fryer oven. Press the Power Button. Cook at 170°F (77°C) for 3 hours, until dry and crisp.
3. Store in a plastic container for up to two weeks.

Air Fried Cinnamon Pears

Prep time: 5 minutes | Cook time: 2 hours | Serves 2

- 2 pears
- 3 tablespoons cinnamon and sugar mixture

1. Line a baking pan with greaseproof paper.
2. Slice the pears very thin and lay them on the pan in a single layer.
3. Sprinkle them with the cinnamon and sugar mixture.
4. Slide the pan into the air fryer oven. Press the Power Button. Cook at 170°F (77°C) for 2 hours, turning pears over halfway through.
5. Transfer to wire rack to cool.

Air Fried Hot Peppers

Prep time: 5 minutes | Cook time: 10 hours | Serves 2

- 10 hot peppers

1. Place the peppers on the air flow racks.
2. Slide the racks into the air fryer oven. Press the Power Button. Cook at 160°F (70°C) for 8 to 10 hours. They should be very dry.

Air Fried Kiwi Chips

Prep time: 5 minutes | Cook time: 6 to 12 hours | Makes 10 to 12 slices

- 2 kiwis

1. Peel the kiwis, using a paring knife to slice the skin off or a vegetable peeler.
2. Slice the peeled kiwis into ¼ inch slices.
3. Place the kiwi slices on the air flow racks. Slide the racks into the air fryer oven. Press the Power Button. Cook at 135°F (57°C) for 6 to 12 hours.
4. These should be slightly chewy when done.

Air Fried Onions

Prep time: 15 minutes | Cook time: 9 hours | Makes 6 tablespoons dried minced onions and 1 tablespoon onion powder

- 1 medium onion

TO DRY THE ONIONS:

1. Prepare your onions by removing the skins, trimming the ends, and slicing into even sized pieces.
2. Separate the onion segments and spread them out evenly on the air flow racks in a single layer.
3. Slide the racks into the air fryer oven. Press the Power Button. Cook at 125°F (52°C) for 3 to 9 hours.
4. The timing will depend on the size of your onion pieces and moisture content. The dehydrated onions should be crisp and snap when your break them.
5. Let the dried onion pieces cool, crush into onion flakes, and package into airtight glass containers or process further into dried onion flakes and onion powder.

Chili Spiced Sweet Bacon

Prep time: 5 minutes | Cook time: 4 hours | Makes 6 slices

- 6 slices bacon
- 3 tablespoons light Demerara sugar
- 2 tablespoons rice vinegar
- 2 tablespoons chili paste
- 1 tablespoon soy sauce

1. Mix Demerara sugar, rice vinegar, chili paste, and soy sauce in a bowl.
2. Add bacon slices and mix until the slices are evenly coated. Marinate for up to 3 hours or until ready to dehydrate.
3. Discard the marinade, and then place the bacon onto the air flow racks. Slide the racks into the air fryer oven. Press the Power Button. Cook at 170°F (77°C) for 4 hours.
4. Remove from the air fryer oven when done and let the bacon cool down for 5 minutes, then serve.

Choco Hazelnut Orange Slices

Prep time: 5 minutes | Cook time: 6 hours | Serves 3

- 2 large oranges cut into ⅛-inch-thick slices
- ½ teaspoon ground star anise
- ½ teaspoon ground cinnamon
- 1 tablespoon chocolate hazelnut spread

1. Sprinkle spices on the orange slices.
2. Place orange slices on the air flow racks. Slide the racks into the air fryer oven. Press the Power Button. Cook at 140°F (60°C) for 6 hours.
3. Remove when done, and if desired serve with chocolate hazelnut spread.

Steamed Lemon Asparagus

Prep time: 5 minutes | Cook time: 5 minutes | Serves 1

- 7 asparagus spears, washed and trimmed
- ¼ teaspoon pepper
- 1 tablespoon extra light olive oil
- Juice from freshly squeezed ¼ lemon
- ¼ teaspoon salt
- 1 cup water

1. Place a trivet or the steamer rack in the Instant Pot and pour in the water.
2. In a mixing bowl, combine the asparagus spears, salt, pepper, and lemon juice.
3. Place on top of the trivet.
4. Lock the lid. Set the Instant Pot to Steam mode, then set the timer for 5 minutes at High Pressure.
5. Once cooking is complete, do a quick pressure release. Carefully open the lid.
6. Drizzle the asparagus with olive oil.

Paprika Broccoli

Prep time: 6 minutes | Cook time: 6 minutes | Serves 2

- ¼ teaspoon ground black pepper
- 1 tablespoon freshly squeezed lemon juice
- ¼ teaspoon salt
- 1 head broccoli, cut into florets
- 1 tablespoon paprika
- 1 cup water

1. Place a trivet or the steamer rack in the Instant Pot and pour in the water.
2. Place the broccoli florets on the trivet and sprinkle salt, pepper, paprika, and lemon juice.
3. Lock the lid. Set the Instant Pot to Steam mode, then set the timer for 6 minutes at High Pressure.
4. Once cooking is complete, do a quick pressure release. Carefully open the lid.
5. Serve immediately.

Brussels Sprout and Pecan Stir-Fry

Prep time: 4 minutes | Cook time: 6 minutes | Serves 4

- ¼ cup chopped pecans
- 2 garlic cloves, minced
- Salt and pepper, to taste
- 2 tablespoons water
- 2 cups baby Brussels sprouts
- 1 tablespoon olive oil

1. Press the Sauté button on the Instant Pot and heat the oil.
2. Sauté the garlic for 1 minute or until fragrant.
3. Add the Brussels sprouts. Sprinkle salt and pepper for seasoning.
4. Add the water.
5. Lock the lid. Set the Instant Pot to Pressure Cook mode, then set the timer for 3 minutes at High Pressure.
6. Once cooking is complete, do a quick pressure release. Carefully open the lid.
7. Add the pecans and set to the Sauté mode and sauté for 3 minutes or until the pecans are roasted.
8. Serve immediately.

Coconut Milk Cabbage

Prep time: 6 minutes | Cook time: 20 minutes | Serves 4

- 2 cups freshly squeezed coconut milk
- 1 halved onion
- 1 thumb-size ginger, sliced
- 1 garlic bulb, crushed
- 1 cabbage head, shredded
- Salt and pepper, to taste

1. In the Instant Pot, add all the ingredients. Stir to mix well.
2. Lock the lid. Set the Instant Pot to Pressure Cook mode, then set the timer for 20 minutes at High Pressure.
3. Once cooking is complete, do a quick pressure release. Carefully open the lid.
4. Serve warm.

Potato and Olive Bowls

Prep time: 15 minutes | Cook time: 40 minutes | Serves 1

- 1 medium russet potatoes, scrubbed and peeled
- 1 teaspoon olive oil
- ¼ teaspoon onion powder
- ⅛ teaspoon salt
- Dollop of butter
- Dollop of cream cheese
- 1 tablespoon Kalamata olives
- 1 tablespoon chopped chives

1. Preheat the Duo Crisp to 200°C.
2. In a bowl, coat the potatoes with the onion powder, salt, olive oil, and butter.
3. Transfer to the Duo Crisp and air fry for 40 minutes, turning the potatoes over at the halfway point.
4. Take care when removing the potatoes from the Duo Crisp and serve with the cream cheese, Kalamata olives and chives on top.

Chapter 8
Starters and Snacks

Banger and Onion Rolls with Mustard
Prep time: 15 minutes | Cook time: 15 minutes | Serves 12

- 1 pound (454 g) bulk breakfast banger
- ½ cup finely chopped onion
- ½ cup fresh bread crumbs
- ½ teaspoon dried mustard
- ½ teaspoon dried sage
- ¼ teaspoon cayenne pepper
- 1 large egg, beaten
- 1 garlic clove, minced
- 2 sheets (1 package) frozen puff pastry, thawed
- plain flour, for dusting

1. In a medium bowl, break up the banger. Stir in the onion, bread crumbs, mustard, sage, cayenne pepper, egg and garlic. Divide the banger mixture in half and tightly wrap each half in Cling Film. Refrigerate for 5 to 10 minutes.
2. Lay the pastry sheets on a lightly floured work surface. Using a rolling pin, lightly roll out the pastry to smooth out the dough. Take out one of the banger packages and form the banger into a long roll. Remove the Cling Film and place the banger on top of the puff pastry about 1 inch from one of the long edges. Roll the pastry around the banger and pinch the edges of the dough together to seal. Repeat with the other pastry sheet and banger.
3. Slice the logs into lengths about 1½ inches long. Place the banger rolls on the sheet pan, cut-side down.
4. Select Roast. Set temperature to 180°C and set time to 15 minutes. Press Start to begin preheating.
5. Once the unit has preheated, place the pan into the Air Fryer.
6. After 7 or 8 minutes, rotate the pan and continue cooking.
7. When cooking is complete, the rolls will be golden brown and sizzling. Remove the pan from the Air Fryer and let cool for 5 minutes.

Chicken Wings with Sriracha Sauce
Prep time: 5 minutes | Cook time: 18 minutes | Serves 4

- 2 pounds (907 g) chicken wings
- 1 tablespoon white vinegar
- Sea salt and ground black pepper, to taste
- 1 teaspoon cayenne pepper
- 1 teaspoon garlic powder
- ½ teaspoon onion powder
- 4 tablespoons butter, room temperature
- ¼ cup Sriracha sauce

1. Start by preheating the air fryer to 190°C.
2. Toss the chicken wings with the remaining ingredients. Transfer to the crisper tray.
3. Place the crisper tray in the corresponding position in the air fryer. Select Roast and cook the chicken wings for 18 minutes, turning them over halfway through the cooking time.
4. Bon appétit!

Wax Beans with Cumin
Prep time: 6 minutes | Cook time: 6 minutes | Serves 4

- 1 pound (454 g) fresh wax beans, trimmed
- 2 teaspoons olive oil
- ½ teaspoon onion powder
- 1 teaspoon garlic powder
- ½ teaspoon cumin powder
- Sea salt and ground black pepper, to taste

1. Start by preheating the air fryer to 200°C.
2. Toss the wax beans with the remaining ingredients. Transfer to the crisper tray.
3. Place the crisper tray in the corresponding position in the air fryer. Select Air Fry and cook the wax beans for about 6 minutes, tossing the crisper tray halfway through the cooking time.
4. Enjoy!

aubergine with Paprika

Prep time: 5 minutes | Cook time: 15 minutes | Serves 3

- ¾ pound (340 g) aubergine
- Sea salt and ground black pepper, to taste
- ½ teaspoon paprika
- 2 tablespoons olive oil
- 2 tablespoons balsamic vinegar

1. Start by preheating the air fryer to 200°C.
2. Toss the aubergine pieces with the remaining ingredients until they are well coated on all sides.
3. Arrange the aubergine in the crisper tray.
4. Place the crisper tray in the corresponding position in the air fryer. Select Air Fry and cook the aubergine for about 15 minutes, shaking the crisper tray halfway through the cooking time.
5. Bon appétit!

Tomato Chips with Cheese

Prep time: 5 minutes | Cook time: 15 minutes | Serves 3

- 1 large-sized beefsteak tomatoes
- 2 tablespoons olive oil
- ½ teaspoon paprika
- Sea salt, to taste
- 1 teaspoon garlic powder
- 1 tablespoon chopped fresh Coriander
- 4 tablespoons grated Pecorino cheese

1. Start by preheating the air fryer to 180°C .
2. Toss the tomato slices with the olive oil and spices until they are well coated on all sides.
3. Arrange the tomato slices in the crisper tray.
4. Place the crisper tray in the corresponding position in the air fryer. Select Air Fry and cook the tomato slices for about 10 minutes.
5. Reduce the temperature to 170°C. Top the tomato slices with the cheese and continue to cook for a further 5 minutes.
6. Bon appétit!

Cinnamon Mixed Nuts

Prep time: 5 minutes | Cook time: 6 minutes | Serves 4

- 1 egg white, lightly beaten
- ½ cup pecan halves
- ½ cup almonds
- ½ cup walnuts
- Sea salt and cayenne pepper, to taste
- 1 teaspoon chili powder
- ½ teaspoon ground cinnamon
- ½ teaspoon ground allspice

1. Start by preheating the air fryer to 170°C.
2. Mix the nuts with the rest of the ingredients and place them in the crisper tray.
3. Place the crisper tray in the corresponding position in the air fryer. Select Air Fry and cook the nuts for 6 minutes, shaking the crisper tray halfway through the cooking time and working in batches.
4. Enjoy!

Paprika beetroot Chips

Prep time: 10 minutes | Cook time: 30 minutes | Serves 2

- ½ pound (227 g) golden beetroots, peeled and thinly sliced
- flake salt and ground black pepper, to taste
- 1 teaspoon paprika
- 2 tablespoons olive oil
- ½ teaspoon garlic powder
- 1 teaspoon ground turmeric

1. Start by preheating the air fryer to 170°C.
2. Toss the beetroots with the remaining ingredients and place them in the crisper tray.
3. Place the crisper tray in the corresponding position in the air fryer. Select Air Fry and cook the chips for 30 minutes, shaking the crisper tray occasionally and working in batches.
4. Enjoy!

Lime Avocado Chips

Prep time: 15 minutes | Cook time: 10 minutes | Serves 4

- 1 egg
- 1 tablespoon lime juice
- ⅛ teaspoon chili sauce
- 2 tablespoons flour
- ¾ cup panko bread crumbs
- ¼ cup cornmeal
- ¼ teaspoon salt
- 1 large avocado, pitted, peeled, and cut into ½-inch slices
- Cooking spray

1. Whisk together the egg, lime juice, and chili sauce in a small bowl.
2. On a sheet of wax paper, place the flour. In a separate sheet of wax paper, combine the bread crumbs, cornmeal, and salt.
3. Dredge the avocado slices one at a time in the flour, then in the egg mixture, finally roll them in the bread crumb mixture to coat well.
4. Place the breaded avocado slices in the air fry basket and mist them with cooking spray.
5. Select Air Fry, set temperature to 200°C, and set time to 10 minutes. Select Start/Stop to begin preheating.
6. Once preheated, place the air fryer basket or wire rack on the air fry position.
7. When cooking is complete, the slices should be nicely browned and crispy. Transfer the avocado slices to a plate and serve.

Sweet and Spicy Roasted Walnuts

Prep time: 5 minutes | Cook time: 15 minutes | Makes 4 cups

- 1 pound (454 g) walnut halves and pieces
- ½ cup granulated sugar
- 3 tablespoons vegetable oil
- 1 teaspoon cayenne pepper
- ½ teaspoon fine salt

1. Soak the walnuts in a large bowl with boiling water for a minute or two. Drain the walnuts. Stir in the sugar, oil and cayenne pepper to coat well. Spread the walnuts in a single layer on the sheet pan.
2. Select Roast, set temperature to 160°C and set time to 15 minutes. Select Start/Stop to begin preheating.
3. When the unit has preheated, place the pan on the roast position.
4. After 7 or 8 minutes, remove the pan from the Air Fryer. Stir the nuts. Return the pan to the Air Fryer and continue cooking, check frequently.
5. When cooking is complete, the walnuts should be dark golden brown. Remove the pan from the Air Fryer. Sprinkle the nuts with the salt and let cool. Serve.

Parma Prosciutto-Wrapped Pears

Prep time: 5 minutes | Cook time: 6 minutes | Serves 8

- 2 large, ripe Anjou pears
- 4 thin slices Parma prosciutto
- 2 teaspoons aged balsamic vinegar

1. Peel the pears. Slice into 8 wedges and cut out the core from each wedge.
2. Cut the prosciutto into 8 long strips. Wrap each pear wedge with a strip of prosciutto. Place the wrapped pears in the sheet pan.
3. Select Broil, set temperature to High and set time to 6 minutes. Select Start/Stop to begin preheating.
4. When the unit has preheated, place the pan on the broil position.
5. After 2 or 3 minutes, check the pears. The pears should be turned over if the prosciutto is beginning to crisp up and brown. Return the pan to the Air Fryer and continue cooking.
6. When cooking is complete, remove the pan from the Air Fryer. Drizzle the pears with the balsamic vinegar and serve warm.

Ricotta Capers with Lemon Zest

Prep time: 10 minutes | Cook time: 8 minutes | Serves 4 to 6

- 1½ cups whole milk ricotta cheese
- 2 tablespoons extra-virgin olive oil
- 2 tablespoons capers, rinsed
- Zest of 1 lemon, plus more for garnish
- 1 teaspoon finely chopped fresh rosemary
- Pinch crushed red pepper flakes
- Salt and freshly ground black pepper, to taste
- 1 tablespoon grated Parmesan cheese

1. In a mixing bowl, stir together the ricotta cheese, olive oil, capers, lemon zest, rosemary, red pepper flakes, salt, and pepper until well combined.
2. Spread the mixture evenly in a baking dish.
3. Select Air Fry, set temperature to 190°C, and set time to 8 minutes. Select Start/Stop to begin preheating.
4. Once preheated, place the baking dish in the Air Fryer.
5. When cooking is complete, the top should be nicely browned. Remove from the Air Fryer and top with a sprinkle of grated Parmesan cheese. Garnish with the lemon zest and serve warm.

Parmesan Ranch Snack Mix

Prep time: 5 minutes | Cook time: 6 minutes | Makes 6 cups

- 2 cups oyster crackers
- 2 cups Chex rice
- 1 cup sesame sticks
- ⅔ cup finely grated Parmesan cheese
- 8 tablespoons unsalted butter, melted
- 1½ teaspoons granulated garlic
- ½ teaspoon flaked salt

1. Toss together all the ingredients in a large bowl until well coated. Spread the mixture on the sheet pan in an even layer.
2. Select Roast, set temperature to 180°C and set time to 6 minutes. Select Start/Stop to begin preheating.
3. When the unit has preheated, place the pan on the roast position.
4. After 3 minutes, remove the pan and stir the mixture. Return the pan to the Air Fryer and continue cooking.
5. When cooking is complete, the mixture should be lightly browned and fragrant. Let cool before serving.

Homemade Potato Chips

Prep time: 5 minutes | Cook time: 22 minutes | Serves 3

- 2 medium potatoes, preferably Yukon Gold, scrubbed
- Cooking spray
- 2 teaspoons olive oil
- ½ teaspoon garlic granules
- ¼ teaspoon paprika
- ¼ teaspoon plus ⅛ teaspoon sea salt
- ¼ teaspoon freshly ground black pepper
- Ketchup or chili sauce, for serving

1. Spritz the air fry basket with cooking spray.
2. On a flat work surface, cut the potatoes into ¼-inch-thick slices. Transfer the potato slices to a medium bowl, along with the olive oil, garlic granules, paprika, salt, and pepper and toss to coat well. Transfer the potato slices to the air fry basket.
3. Select Air Fry, set temperature to 392°F (200°C), and set time to 22 minutes. Select Start/Stop to begin preheating.
4. Once preheated, place the air fryer basket or wire rack on the air fry position. Stir the potato slices twice during the cooking process.
5. When cooking is complete, the potato chips should be tender and nicely browned. Remove from the Air Fryer and serve alongside the ketchup for dipping.

Cinnamon Apple Wedges with Yogurt

Prep time: 5 minutes | Cook time: 12 minutes | Serves 4

- 2 medium apples, cored and sliced into ¼-inch wedges
- 1 teaspoon rapeseed oil
- 2 teaspoons peeled and grated fresh ginger
- ½ teaspoon ground cinnamon
- ½ cup low-fat Greek vanilla yogurt, for serving

1. In a large bowl, toss the apple wedges with the rapeseed oil, ginger, and cinnamon until evenly coated. Put the apple wedges in the air fry basket.
2. Select Air Fry, set temperature to 180°C , and set time to 12 minutes. Select Start/Stop to begin preheating.
3. Once preheated, place the air fryer basket or wire rack on the air fry position.
4. When cooking is complete, the apple wedges should be crisp-tender. Remove the apple wedges from the Air Fryer and serve drizzled with the yogurt.

Air-Fried Old Bay Chicken Wings

Prep time: 5 minutes | Cook time: 13 minutes | Serves 4

- 2 tablespoons Old Bay seasoning
- 2 teaspoons baking powder
- 2 teaspoons salt
- 2 pounds (907 g) chicken wings, patted dry
- Cooking spray

1. Combine the Old Bay seasoning, baking powder, and salt in a large zip-top plastic bag. Add the chicken wings, seal, and shake until the wings are thoroughly coated in the seasoning mixture.
2. Lightly spray the air fry basket with cooking spray. Lay the chicken wings in the air fry basket in a single layer and lightly mist them with cooking spray.
3. Select Air Fry, set temperature to 200°C, and set time to 13 minutes. Select Start/Stop to begin preheating.
4. Once preheated, place the air fryer basket or wire rack on the air fry position. Flip the wings halfway through the cooking time.
5. When cooking is complete, the wings should reach an internal temperature of 75°C on a meat thermometer. Remove from the Air Fryer to a plate and serve hot.

Simple Carrot Chips

Prep time: 5 minutes | Cook time: 10 minutes | Serves 4

- 4 to 5 medium carrots, trimmed and thinly sliced
- 1 tablespoon olive oil, plus more for greasing
- 1 teaspoon seasoned salt

1. Toss the carrot slices with 1 tablespoon of olive oil and salt in a medium bowl until thoroughly coated.
2. Grease the air fry basket with the olive oil. Place the carrot slices in the greased pan.
3. Select Air Fry, set temperature to 200°C, and set time to 10 minutes. Select Start/Stop to begin preheating.
4. Once preheated, place the air fryer basket or wire rack on the air fry position. Stir the carrot slices halfway through the cooking time.
5. When cooking is complete, the chips should be crisp-tender. Remove the air fryer basket or wire rack from the Air Fryer and allow to cool for 5 minutes before serving.

Sesame Kale Chips

Prep time: 15 minutes | Cook time: 8 minutes | Serves 5

- 8 cups deribbed kale leaves, torn into 2-inch pieces
- 1½ tablespoons olive oil
- ¾ teaspoon chili powder
- ¼ teaspoon garlic powder
- ½ teaspoon paprika
- 2 teaspoons sesame seeds

1. In a large bowl, toss the kale with the olive oil, chili powder, garlic powder, paprika, and sesame seeds until well coated.
2. Transfer the kale to the air fry basket.
3. Select Air Fry, set temperature to 180°C, and set time to 8 minutes. Select Start/Stop to begin preheating.
4. Once preheated, place the air fryer basket or wire rack on the air fry position. Flip the kale twice during cooking.
5. When cooking is complete, the kale should be crispy. Remove from the Air Fryer and serve warm.

Dehydrated Strawberries

Prep time: 10 minutes | Cook time: 2 hours | Serves 4

- 1 pound (454 g) fresh strawberries

1. Line three air flow racks with greaseproof paper.
2. Wash strawberries and cut off stem ends. Cut strawberries into slices, about ⅛ inch thick.
3. Place sliced strawberries on the air flow racks. Space them so the pieces are not touching.
4. Slide the racks into the air fryer oven. Press the Power Button. Cook at 170°F (77°C) for 30 minutes. Use tongs to turn the berries. Cook for another 30 minutes. Repeat this until strawberry slices are leathery.
5. Allow the slices to cool completely. Transfer dried strawberry slices to an airtight container. They will keep up to 5 days.

Peach Fruit Leather

Prep time: 15 minutes | Cook time: 6 hours 15 minutes | Serves 4

- 4 peaches, pitted and each peach cut into 6 pieces

1. Line three air flow racks with greaseproof paper. Place peach slices on parchment.
2. Slide the racks into the air fryer oven. Press the Power Button. Cook at 200°C for 15 minutes.
3. Transfer the cooked peaches to a blender or food processor and blend until smooth.
4. Line a baking tray with greaseproof paper and pour peach purée onto paper, spreading as necessary with a spatula into an even layer.
5. Slide the sheet into the air fryer oven. Press the Power Button. Cook at 130°F (54°C) for 6 hours or until leather is desired consistency.

Smoky Venison Jerky

Prep time: 30 minutes | Cook time: 4 hours | Makes 1 to 2 pounds

- 3 to 5 pounds (1.4 to 2.3 kg) deer roast
- Hi-Mountain cure and jerky mix or another brand
- 3 to 5 teaspoons liquid smoke

1. Start by slicing your roast into thin strips, and removing any silver skin on each piece of the meat.
2. Lay it all out flat, and then mix up your seasoning per the box. Sprinkle on both sides of the meat, massaging it in.
3. Then transfer the meat into a bag and add in the liquid smoke. Massage bag.
4. Store in the fridge for 24 hours to let it marinade and cure.
5. Lay the jerky out on the air flow racks, don't let the pieces touch.
6. Slide the racks into the air fryer oven. Press the Power Button. Cook at 160°F (70°C) for 3 to 4 hours.
7. Make sure to flip and randomly check, and remove the meat when it is cooked to your texture liking.

Dried Mushrooms

Prep time: 30 minutes | Cook time: 4 hours | Makes 2½ quarts

- 4 to 5 pounds (1.8 to 2.3 kg) fresh mushrooms, washed, rinsed and drained well.

1. Rinse whole mushrooms well under cold running water. Gently scrub any visible dirt away with out damaging the mushroom. Pat dry with kitchen paper if needed.
2. Break the stem off of each mushroom and slice into ¼ to ½ inch thick slices with a sharp knife.
3. Place the sliced mushrooms on the parchment-lined air flow racks.
4. Slide the racks into the air fryer oven. Press the Power Button. Cook at 170°F (77°C) for 4 hours.
5. Check the mushrooms after 1 hour and flip them over for even drying. Check the mushroom slices every hour.
6. As the mushroom slices dry, remove them from the air fryer oven and allow to cool on the racks or a paper towel.
7. Store dried mushroom slices in an airtight glass container.

Dehydrated courgette Chips

Prep time: 10 minutes | Cook time: 3 hours | Serves 4

- 4 to 5 medium courgette, thinly sliced
- 2 tablespoons olive oil
- Garlic salt and black pepper, to taste

1. Toss the courgette with the olive oil, garlic salt and pepper.
2. Lay in a single layer on the air flow racks. Slide the racks into the air fryer oven. Press the Power Button. Cook at 170°F (77°C) for 3 hours, until dry and crisp.
3. Store in a plastic container for up to two weeks.

Chapter 9
Fast and Easy Everyday Favourites

Vanilla Cinnamon Toast

Prep time: 5 minutes | Cook time: 5 minutes | Serves 6

- 1½ teaspoons cinnamon
- 1½ teaspoons vanilla extract
- ½ cup sugar
- 2 teaspoons ground black pepper
- 2 tablespoons melted coconut oil
- 12 slices whole wheat bread

1. Combine all the ingredients, except for the bread, in a large bowl. Stir to mix well.
2. Dunk the bread in the bowl of mixture gently to coat and infuse well. Shake the excess off. Arrange the bread slices in the air fry basket.
3. Select Air Fry , set temperature to 200°C and set time to 5 minutes. Select Start/Stop to begin preheating.
4. Once the oven has preheated, place the air fryer basket or wire rack on the air fry position. Flip the bread halfway through.
5. When cooking is complete, the bread should be golden brown.
6. Remove the bread slices from the oven and slice to serve.

Parmesan Prawns

Prep time: 10 minutes | Cook time: 8 minutes | Serves 4 to 6

- ⅔ cup grated Parmesan cheese
- 4 minced garlic cloves
- 1 teaspoon onion powder
- ½ teaspoon oregano
- 1 teaspoon basil
- 1 teaspoon ground black pepper
- 2 tablespoons olive oil
- 2 pounds (907 g) cooked large Prawns, peeled and deveined
- Lemon wedges, for topping
- Cooking spray

1. Spritz the air fry basket with cooking spray.
2. Combine all the ingredients, except for the Prawns, in a large bowl. Stir to mix well.
3. Dunk the Prawns in the mixture and toss to coat well. Shake the excess off. Arrange the Prawns in the air fry basket.
4. Select Air Fry, set temperature to 180°C and set time to 8 minutes. Select Start/Stop to begin preheating.
5. Once the oven has preheated, place the air fryer basket or wire rack on the air fry position. Flip the Prawns halfway through the cooking time.
6. When cooking is complete, the Prawns should be opaque. Remove the pan from the oven.
7. Transfer the cooked Prawns on a large plate and squeeze the lemon wedges over before serving.

Manchego Cheese Wafers

Prep time: 5 minutes | Cook time: 5 minutes | Serves 2

- 1 cup shredded aged Manchego cheese
- 1 teaspoon plain flour
- ½ teaspoon cumin seeds
- ¼ teaspoon cracked black pepper

1. Line the air fry basket with greaseproof paper.
2. Combine the cheese and flour in a bowl. Stir to mix well. Spread the mixture in the air fryer basket or wire rack into a 4-inch round.
3. Combine the cumin and black pepper in a small bowl. Stir to mix well. Sprinkle the cumin mixture over the cheese round.
4. Select Air Fry, set temperature to 190°C and set time to 5 minutes. Select Start/Stop to begin preheating.
5. Once preheated, place the air fryer basket or wire rack on the air fry position.
6. When cooked, the cheese will be lightly browned and frothy.
7. Use tongs to transfer the cheese wafer onto a plate and slice to serve.

Cherry Tomato with Basil

Prep time: 5 minutes | Cook time: 5 minutes | Serves 2

- 2 cups cherry tomatoes
- 1 clove garlic, thinly sliced
- 1 teaspoon olive oil
- ⅛ teaspoon flaked salt
- 1 tablespoon freshly chopped basil, for topping
- Cooking spray

1. Spritz a baking pan with cooking spray and set aside.
2. In a large bowl, toss together the cherry tomatoes, sliced garlic, olive oil, and flaked salt. Spread the mixture in an even layer in the prepared pan.
3. Select Bake, set temperature to 180°C and set time to 5 minutes. Select Start/Stop to begin preheating.
4. Once the oven has preheated, place the pan on the bake position.
5. When cooking is complete, the tomatoes should be the soft and wilted.
6. Transfer to a bowl and rest for 5 minutes. Top with the chopped basil and serve warm.

Prawn, Banger and Corn Bake

Prep time: 10 minutes | Cook time: 18 minutes | Serves 2

- 1 ear corn, husk and silk removed, cut into 2-inch rounds
- 8 ounces (227 g) red potatoes, unpeeled, cut into 1-inch pieces
- 2 teaspoons Old Bay Seasoning, divided
- 2 teaspoons vegetable oil, divided
- ¼ teaspoon ground black pepper
- 8 ounces (227 g) large Prawns (about 12 Prawns), deveined
- 6 ounces (170 g) andouille or chorizo banger, cut into 1-inch pieces
- 2 garlic cloves, minced
- 1 tablespoon chopped fresh parsley

1. Put the corn rounds and potatoes in a large bowl. Sprinkle with 1 teaspoon of Old Bay seasoning and drizzle with vegetable oil. Toss to coat well.
2. Transfer the corn rounds and potatoes onto a baking pan.
3. Select Bake, set temperature to 200°C and set time to 18 minutes. Select Start/Stop to begin preheating.
4. Once preheated, place the pan on the bake position.
5. After 6 minutes, remove the pan from the oven. Stir the corn rounds and potatoes. Return the pan to the oven and continue cooking.
6. Meanwhile, cut slits into the Prawns but be careful not to cut them through. Combine the Prawns, banger, remaining Old Bay seasoning, and remaining vegetable oil in the large bowl. Toss to coat well.
7. After 6 minutes, remove the pan from the oven. Add the Prawns and banger to the pan. Return the pan to the oven and continue cooking for 6 minutes. Stir the Prawn mixture halfway through the cooking time.
8. When done, the Prawns should be opaque. Remove the pan from the oven.
9. Transfer the dish to a plate and spread with parsley before serving.

Chips with Lemony Cream Dip

Prep time: 10 minutes | Cook time: 15 minutes | Serves 2 to 4

- 2 large russet potatoes, sliced into ⅛-inch slices, rinsed
- Sea salt and freshly ground black pepper, to taste
- Cooking spray
- Lemony Cream Dip:
- ½ cup Soured cream
- ¼ teaspoon lemon juice
- 2 scallions, white part only, minced
- 1 tablespoon olive oil
- ¼ teaspoon salt
- Freshly ground black pepper, to taste

1. Soak the potato slices in water for 10 minutes, then pat dry with kitchen paper.
2. Transfer the potato slices in the air fry basket. Spritz the slices with cooking spray.
3. Select Air Fry, set temperature to 150°C and set time to 15 minutes. Select Start/Stop to begin preheating.
4. Once the oven has preheated, place the air fryer basket or wire rack on the air fry position. Stir the potato slices three times during cooking. Sprinkle with salt and ground black pepper in the last minute.
5. Meanwhile, combine the ingredients for the dip in a small bowl. Stir to mix well.
6. When cooking is complete, the potato slices will be crispy and golden brown. Remove the air fryer basket or wire rack from the oven.
7. Serve the potato chips immediately with the dip.

Air-Fried Brussels Sprouts

Prep time: 5 minutes | Cook time: 20 minutes | Serves 4

- ¼ teaspoon salt
- ⅛ teaspoon ground black pepper
- 1 tablespoon extra-virgin olive oil
- 1 pound (454 g) Brussels sprouts, trimmed and halved
- Lemon wedges, for garnish

1. Combine the salt, black pepper, and olive oil in a large bowl. Stir to mix well.
2. Add the Brussels sprouts to the bowl of mixture and toss to coat well. Arrange the Brussels sprouts in the air fry basket.
3. Select Air Fry, set temperature to 180°C and set time to 20 minutes. Select Start/Stop to begin preheating.
4. Once preheated, place the air fryer basket or wire rack on the air fry position. Stir the Brussels sprouts two times during cooking.
5. When cooked, the Brussels sprouts will be lightly browned and wilted. Remove from the oven.
6. Transfer the cooked Brussels sprouts to a large plate and squeeze the lemon wedges on top to serve.

Buttered Knots with Parsley

Prep time: 5 minutes | Cook time: 5 minutes | Makes 8 knots

- 1 teaspoon dried parsley
- ¼ cup melted butter
- 2 teaspoons garlic powder
- 1 (11-ounce / 312-g) tube refrigerated French bread dough, cut into 8 slices

1. Combine the parsley, butter, and garlic powder in a bowl. Stir to mix well.
2. Place the French bread dough slices on a clean work surface, then roll each slice into a 6-inch long rope. Tie the ropes into knots and arrange them on a plate.
3. Transfer the knots into a baking pan. Brush the knots with butter mixture.
4. Select Air Fry , set temperature to 180°C and set time to 5 minutes. Select Start/Stop to begin preheating.
5. Once the oven has preheated, slide the pan into the oven. Flip the knots halfway through the cooking time.
6. When done, the knots should be golden brown. Remove the pan from the oven.
7. Serve immediately.

Okra Chips

Prep time: 5 minutes | Cook time: 16 minutes | Serves 6

- 2 pounds (907 g) fresh okra pods, cut into 1-inch pieces
- 2 tablespoons rapeseed oil
- 1 teaspoon coarse sea salt

1. Stir the oil and salt in a bowl to mix well. Add the okra and toss to coat well. Place the okra in the air fry basket.
2. Select Air Fry, set temperature to 200°C and set time to 16 minutes. Select Start/Stop to begin preheating.
3. Once the oven has preheated, place the air fryer basket or wire rack on the air fry position. Flip the okra at least three times during cooking.
4. When cooked, the okra should be lightly browned. Remove from the oven.
5. Serve immediately.

Bacon-Wrapped Jalapeño Poppers

Prep time: 5 minutes | Cook time: 12 minutes | Serves 6

- 6 large jalapeños
- 4 ounces (113 g) ⅓-less-fat cream cheese
- ¼ cup shredded reduced-fat sharp Cheddar cheese
- 2 scallions, green tops only, sliced
- 6 slices center-cut bacon, halved

1. Preheat the air fryer oven to 160°C.
2. Wearing rubber gloves, halve the jalapeños lengthwise to make 12 pieces. Scoop out the seeds and membranes and discard.
3. In a medium bowl, combine the cream cheese, Cheddar, and scallions. Using a small spoon or spatula, fill the jalapeños with the cream cheese filling. Wrap a bacon strip around each pepper and secure with a toothpick.
4. Working in batches, place the stuffed peppers in a single layer in the air fryer basket or wire rack. Select Bake with Convection, and cook for about 12 minutes, until the peppers are tender, the bacon is browned and crisp, and the cheese is melted.
5. Serve warm.

Easy Devils on Horseback

Prep time: 5 minutes | Cook time: 7 minutes | Serves 12

- 24 petite pitted prunes (4½ ounces / 128 g)
- ¼ cup crumbled blue cheese, divided
- 8 slices center-cut bacon, cut crosswise into thirds

1. Preheat the air fryer oven to 200°C.
2. Halve the prunes lengthwise, but don't cut them all the way through. Place ½ teaspoon of cheese in the center of each prune. Wrap a piece of bacon around each prune and secure the bacon with a toothpick.
3. Working in batches, arrange a single layer of the prunes in the air fryer basket or wire rack. Air fry for about 7 minutes, flipping halfway, until the bacon is cooked through and crisp.
4. Let cool slightly and serve warm.

Classic Mexican Street Corn

Prep time: 5 minutes | Cook time: 7 minutes | Serves 4

- 4 medium ears corn, husked
- Cooking spray
- 2 tablespoons mayonnaise
- 1 tablespoon fresh lime juice
- ½ teaspoon ancho chile powder
- ¼ teaspoon flaked salt
- 2 ounces (57 g) crumbled Cotija or feta cheese
- 2 tablespoons chopped fresh Coriander

1. Preheat the air fryer oven to 190°C.
2. Spritz the corn with cooking spray. Working in batches, arrange the ears of corn in the air fryer basket or wire rack in a single layer. Air fry for about 7 minutes, flipping halfway, until the kernels are tender when pierced with a paring knife. When cool enough to handle, cut the corn kernels off the cob.
3. In a large bowl, mix together mayonnaise, lime juice, ancho powder, and salt. Add the corn kernels and mix to combine. Transfer to a serving dish and top with the Cotija and Coriander. Serve immediately.

Appendix 1 Measurement Conversion Chart

Volume Equivalents (Dry)

US STANDARD	METRIC (APPROXIMATE)
1/8 teaspoon	0.5 mL
1/4 teaspoon	1 mL
1/2 teaspoon	2 mL
3/4 teaspoon	4 mL
1 teaspoon	5 mL
1 tablespoon	15 mL
1/4 cup	59 mL
1/2 cup	118 mL
3/4 cup	177 mL
1 cup	235 mL
2 cups	475 mL
3 cups	700 mL
4 cups	1 L

Weight Equivalents

US STANDARD	METRIC (APPROXIMATE)
1 ounce	28 g
2 ounces	57 g
5 ounces	142 g
10 ounces	284 g
15 ounces	425 g
16 ounces (1 pound)	455 g
1.5 pounds	680 g
2 pounds	907 g

Volume Equivalents (Liquid)

US STANDARD	US STANDARD (OUNCES)	METRIC (APPROXIMATE)
2 tablespoons	1 fl.oz.	30 mL
1/4 cup	2 fl.oz.	60 mL
1/2 cup	4 fl.oz.	120 mL
1 cup	8 fl.oz.	240 mL
1 1/2 cup	12 fl.oz.	355 mL
2 cups or 1 pint	16 fl.oz.	475 mL
4 cups or 1 quart	32 fl.oz.	1 L
1 gallon	128 fl.oz.	4 L

Temperatures Equivalents

FAHRENHEIT(F)	CELSIUS(C) APPROXIMATE)
225 °F	107 °C
250 °F	120 ° °C
275 °F	135 °C
300 °F	150 °C
325 °F	160 °C
350 °F	180 °C
375 °F	190 °C
400 °F	205 °C
425 °F	220 °C
450 °F	235 °C
475 °F	245 °C
500 °F	260 °C

Appendix 2 The Dirty Dozen and Clean Fifteen

The Environmental Working Group (EWG) is a nonprofit, nonpartisan organization dedicated to protecting human health and the environment Its mission is to empower people to live healthier lives in a healthier environment. This organization publishes an annual list of the twelve kinds of produce, in sequence, that have the highest amount of pesticide residue-the Dirty Dozen-as well as a list of the fifteen kinds ofproduce that have the least amount of pesticide residue-the Clean Fifteen.

THE DIRTY DOZEN	
The 2016 Dirty Dozen includes the following produce. These are considered among the year's most important produce to buy organic:	
Strawberries	Spinach
Apples	Tomatoes
Nectarines	Bell peppers
Peaches	Cherry tomatoes
Celery	Cucumbers
Grapes	Kale/collard greens
Cherries	Hot peppers

The Dirty Dozen list contains two additional itemskale/collard greens and hot peppers-because they tend to contain trace levels of highly hazardous pesticides.

THE CLEAN FIFTEEN	
The least critical to buy organically are the Clean Fifteen list. The following are on the 2016 list:	
Avocados	Papayas
Corn	Kiw
Pineapples	Eggplant
Cabbage	Honeydew
Sweet peas	Grapefruit
Onions	Cantaloupe
Asparagus	Cauliflower
Mangos	

Some of the sweet corn sold in the United States are made from genetically engineered (GE) seedstock. Buy organic varieties of these crops to avoid GE produce.

Appendix 3 Index

DIANE J. BRANCH

Printed in Great Britain
by Amazon

15966959R00054